WESTERN EUROPE

SINCE THE WAR

A Short Political History

JACQUES FREYMOND

FREDERICK A. PRAEGER, *Publisher*

New York • London

FREDERICK A. PRAEGER, PUBLISHER
64 UNIVERSITY PLACE, NEW YORK 3, N.Y., U.S.A.
77–79 CHARLOTTE STREET, LONDON W. 1, ENGLAND

Published in the United States of America in 1964 by
Frederick A. Praeger, Inc., Publisher

Printed in the United States of America

Preface

At the end of World War II, the European nations were faced
with an urgent problem: What could fill the vacuum created
by the dissolution of the Third Reich and the disintegration
of the European system? France, emerging from a long and
demoralizing occupation, did not have the means—and Italy
even less so. Great Britain, rightly proud of her great contribution to the final victory, was drained and exhausted. The
United States and the Soviet Union, therefore, had the field to
themselves and, in fact, were already occupying it. The meeting of American and Soviet troops at the Elbe was no mere
symbol: Europe was a defenseless pawn in the hands of these
two colossal powers. The conflict in which these two great
powers were opposed entailed the complete division of the
European continent. On either side of the frontier that the
war had created, two new Europes began their new lives—one
Soviet, one Atlantic.

It is the history of Atlantic Europe that is traced in this
essay. It is the history of a long and difficult struggle to recover
from bankruptcy, to regain and re-form a European strength,
and to refine the new Europe in relation to the Soviet chal-

lenge and to her American ally and protector. The European
recovery—a development so remarkable that today it is difficult to recall how tragic, indeed desperate, the situation
seemed in 1945—was not without anxiety or dissension. Atlantic Europe is so diverse that within it everyone considered
its problems (and still does) from a different perspective. And
it is so profoundly integrated in the Atlantic world that Europeans find it difficult to mark a definite boundary or limit to
their efforts. This results in frequent stormy discussions among
member states and with Atlantic partners; in Europe's wavering indecision; her alternation of audacious initiative and suddenly arrested action, of checks and new beginnings; and
finally, in her uneasiness, which persists despite her success
and new-found strength. The European structure appears
fragile still, in a world dominated by nuclear power and
troubled with still unresolved dilemmas.

Yet the Atlantic Europe of 1963 is equipped with great
economic power and an urgent dynamism that is the envy of
its adversaries. It has become the living proof that speaks for
the authors of the Grand Design. But in Berlin, the two colossal powers still confront each other.

The study of contemporary affairs poses many problems for
the historian who does not have access to the sort of archives
available for earlier periods. I have tried to make up for this
lack by using the relatively large resources of available published material. Actually, it is less difficult than one might
imagine to trace government politics and policies, since so
many official declarations and documents are being published.
As for the fluctuations in public opinion, it is not impossible
to follow them in the press, from the polls, and by means of
"soundings" made from time to time. Lastly, I have in my
possession various personal "archives," particularly of pam-
phlets, documents, and other material of limited circulation.
Nevertheless, I must emphasize that I have written a histor-

ical essay, not a history of contemporary Europe. Several parts of it have already appeared in Volume X of the *Propyläen Weltgeschichte* and are reproduced here with the kind permission of the publisher. Chapter 9, "1961: A Year of Crisis," appeared in the *Annuaire européen 1961* (The Hague: Martinus Nijhoff, 1962).

I have appended a bibliography listing all the works referred to in the text itself. Those who wish to investigate more systematically the studies made on this period of European history might refer to several other recent bibliographies: *The Atlantic Community: An Introductory Bibliography*, prepared by the Conference on Atlantic Community (2 vols.; Leyden: A. W. Sythoff, 1961); *Bibliographie européenne*, prepared by the Association des Instituts d'Etudes européennes, in *Bulletin du Centre européen de la Culture: 1954*, No. 5; *L'Edition et l'Europe; Nouvelle bibliographie européenne*, in *Bulletin du Centre européen de la Culture: 1963*, No. 4. (Another bibliography is planned for publication in 1964.)

Lastly, I should like to express my gratitude to those persons who so kindly offered information and advice: M. Denis de Rougemont, Director of the Centre européen de la Culture and one of the most knowledgeable writers about the history of the European Movement; M. Henri Schwamm, Secretary General of the Centre; and M. Pierre Pagneux, Librarian at the Graduate Institute of International Studies at Geneva.

JACQUES FREYMOND

Geneva
October, 1962

Contents

Preface   v

1. Where Is Europe?   3
2. First Efforts   29
3. From European Unity to the Atlantic Pact   50
4. Stormy Dialogues Across the Atlantic   73
5. Europe in Crisis: 1952–54   92
6. Suez and Budapest   112
7. Europe's Resurgence   128
8. Economic Progress and Political Complications: 1959–60   152
9. 1961: A Year of Crisis   173
10. The Grand Design Debated: 1962   200

Epilogue   216
A Selected Bibliography   223
Name Index   229
Subject Index   232

WESTERN EUROPE
SINCE THE WAR

{ 1 }

Where Is Europe?

Twenty-eight centuries of Europe! The title of a recent work* evokes the depth of history upon which the architects of contemporary Europe must build.

No one doubts that a common consciousness of European civilization, even of a European state system, may have existed in past centuries. But the system, homogeneous as it was, was marked by continuous rivalry among the powers. Europe was only a geographic expression, a land mass constantly fought over by Hohenstaufen, Capetien, and Plantagenet, by Hapsburg and Bourbon, by France, Great Britain, Austria, Russia, Prussia, and Germany, in perpetual readjustment of a precarious balance, a peninsula from which the great powers spread out to other continents, which, in turn, they divided and finally involved in their intra-European struggles.

It was precisely this process that was to cause the destruction of these powers. Finally, after two world wars, in the course of which certain nations established their hegemony across the continent, the European nations were forced to

---

* Denis de Rougemont, *Vingt-huit siècles d'Europe: La conscience européenne à travers les textes d'Hésiode à nos jours* (Paris: Payot, 1961).

realize not only the possibility but the necessity of a "European" policy.

The awakening had been slow. There were few who had recognized immediately the revolutionary effects of World War I. The order established at Versailles was therefore fragile, not because the treaties were intrinsically bad, but because they did not correspond to real power relationships after 1920. The break-up of the great coalition that had defeated the Central Powers placed upon France the entire burden of resisting movements for change in the European balance. And the French system of flank alliances was only a poor substitute for the security system devised with American and British participation. The states included in it—bound together though they were by fear of a Hapsburg restoration, fear of German revenge, and fear of Bolshevism—were too weak, dispersed, and busy with the defense of their immediate interests to overcome the infantile diseases of nationalism and thereby play a catalytic role in Eastern Europe. And France, which could count on them only insofar as she was ready to support them, became progressively less alert to the strategic obligations that the system imposed on her. Munich, which came at the end of a process of evolution marked by the rearmament of Germany and the remilitarization of the Rhineland, made the contradiction between "offensive" diplomacy and "defensive" strategy unmistakably clear.

The disequilibrium of the balance of power was just as obvious on a global scale. Certainly France and Great Britain, the two European powers of world influence, still created an illusion of strength; the division of spoils from the conquered nations had even permitted them to reinforce their positions. But the upsurge of anticolonial nationalism—fed as it was by principles the mother countries called their own, by the preaching of Wilsonism, and by the action of the Communist International—did not cease. The colonial empires, however imposing they appeared, were in fact crumbling from within.

The wide geographical dispersal of their lands might have furnished France and England with the means to make their influence felt on a worldwide scale. But on the contrary, the imperial will had weakened, and both countries refused to take the risks that power requires to be made, thereby increasing the vulnerability of their possessions spread around the globe. Great Britain and France were incapable of resisting Japanese activities in China, not because they lacked the means to do so, but because they did not care to apply them. Their expectation that the United States would intervene was in itself an admission of their own inability to guard the established order. And American abstention only underlined more harshly still the vacuum on the world political scene caused by this failure on the part of the Western powers.

Of the three powers that had led the allied coalition to victory in 1918, one had taken refuge in the illusions of isolationism; the two others—unsure, hesitant, and therefore incapable of agreeing on a common policy—contented themselves with conserving what they already had. They were no longer able, either in Europe or in the world at large, to resist the forces of aggression or the advancements made by opponents of the established order. Nor did they any longer provide sufficient counterweight to the threat that was finally to coalesce in an alliance between Nazi Germany, Fascist Italy, and Japan—the new, conquering empires whose activities opened the way for the revolutionary action of the Soviet Union and the colonial peoples.

Thus Europe let herself slide once again into a military conflagration in which she involved the entire world. She did so through cowardice, but also through vanity and lack of imagination. One has heard it said: *"Nous autres civilisations, nous savons maintenant que nous sommes mortelles."* Was this now true of Europe? The political elite on whom the defense of Western civilization depended never thought to apply this reflection to themselves. The men responsible for the conduct of European affairs between the two wars, gifted as many of them were, had allowed themselves to become imprisoned in a generalized mediocrity. Valid proposals were drowned in verbalisms incanted by magicians of peace, and neither the Wall Street crash nor the Mukden incident nor the rise of Hitler incited the governments to take seriously Briand's proposals for creating an association of European states. The initiatives of Coudenhove-Kalergi met with only a limited response. Churchill, who had published an article in favor of European political association as early as 1930,* was an isolated exception.

But Churchill had no better luck when, as Prime Minister, on June 16, 1940, he submitted a proposal for a Franco-British Union to the French Government. It was not, as he saw it, merely a question of strengthening a wartime alliance, but of creating an indissoluble union of the two countries:

> At this most fateful moment in the history of the modern world, the Governments of the United Kingdom and the French Republic make this declaration of indissoluble union and unyielding resolution in their common defence of justice and freedom against subjection to a system which reduces mankind to a life of robots and slaves.
>
> The two Governments declare that France and Great Britain shall no longer be two nations, but one Franco-British Union.
>
> The constitution of the Union will provide for joint organs of defence, foreign, financial, and economic policies.
>
> Every citizen of France will enjoy immediately citizenship of Great Britain; every British subject will become a citizen of France.
>
> Both countries will share responsibility for the repair of the devastation of war, wherever it occurs in their territories, and the resources of both shall be equally, and as one, applied to that purpose.
>
> During the war there shall be a single War Cabinet, and all the forces of Britain and France, whether on land, sea, or in the

---

* "The United States of Europe," *The Saturday Evening Post*, February 15, 1930.

air, will be placed under its direction. It will govern from wherever it best can. The two Parliaments will be formally associated. The nations of the British Empire are already forming new armies. France will keep her available forces in the field, on the sea, and in the air. The Union appeals to the United States to fortify the economic resources of the Allies, and to bring her powerful material aid to the common cause.

The Union will concentrate its whole energy against the power of the enemy, no matter where the battle may be.

And thus we shall conquer.*

The project, it will be noted, was as revolutionary as the circumstances in which it was proposed. Faced with the formidable demonstration of Nazi Germany's power, England and France could no longer be content merely to join forces in opposition: A veritable fusion was necessary. This is exactly what a man like Arnold Toynbee foresaw from the very beginning of the war, when he wrote to Etienne Dennery, General Secretary of the Foreign Policy Center in Paris, on September 16, 1939: "I am under the impression that if France and England do not come to a *rapprochement* that will permit them, so to speak, to be a single country, it is inevitable that the unification of Europe will come about one day or another in the form of German domination exercised over our two countries."†

Toynbee went on to propose a methodical study of how to strengthen the ties between the two countries, so that the future European Union would be founded on the "ideas and traditions" of France and England. This study was, in fact, made. Two committees were created in London and Paris

* See Winston S. Churchill, *The Second World War*, Vol. II: *Their Finest Hour* (London: Cassell & Company, 1949; Boston: Houghton Mifflin Co., 1950), pp. 219–20.

† *Ibid.*, pp. 183–84. See also Léon Noël, "Le Projet d'union franco-britannique de juin 1940," *La Revue d'histoire de la deuxième guerre mondiale*, January, 1956, pp. 22–37. There are several subtle differences between the text as it appears in the Churchill history and in the Noël article. The latter text is that which General de Gaulle transmitted to Paul Reynaud.

during the winter of 1939–40, in which discussions of the
eventual Franco-British Union were carried on.

The initiative for Churchill's proposal for the Franco-
British Union did not, however, come from these circles. The
impetus came from another group, one more directly involved
in politics.* It was M. Monick, Financial Attaché at the
French Embassy in London, who, struck by the ideas advanced
by Clarence Streit and the proposals for Atlantic union, had
seen in a union of France and England the first step toward
Atlantic union. He had discussed this with the French Ambassador, Charles Corbin, and with Jean Monnet, then President of the Franco-British Economic Coordination Committee.
Monnet, in turn, had gone to Sir Robert Vansittart, then chief
diplomatic adviser to the Foreign Secretary, and to General de
Gaulle, upon the latter's arrival in London on June 10. De
Gaulle, like Churchill, who was informed simultaneously, was
sufficiently aware of the dimensions of Europe's present catastrophe to take up the idea immediately; it was formally presented as a proposal that, after acceptance by the British
Cabinet, was officially transmitted to Bordeaux.

The revolutionary proposal testifies to its authors' breadth
of vision. But it fell on ground that was ill prepared to receive
it. Too much rancor had accumulated in the equivocations
that had characterized Franco-British relations between the
two wars. France was tired, shocked by events for which she
had been unprepared. The men in power were already resigned, and they inclined toward acceptance of a defeat they
considered inevitable. Those who, like General de Gaulle, had
pressed Churchill and the British Government for a declaration of union—which, they thought, would fire the imagination and renew the national energy of France—were a small
and relatively isolated group.

Thus Britain was left alone, to become the nucleus of re-

* See Noël, *loc. cit.*

sistance to a machine bent on destroying European civilization and to gather about her the remaining forces who understood what was at stake.

For a few short years, Hitler's Germany reigned on the Continent, which was reorganized and mobilized to support her war effort. But she never dominated it. On the contrary, the methods she used to reduce Europe to slavery provoked world-wide opposition, and, their very existence threatened, the European nations reacted by affirming their will to live and endure. The unity of Europe, which the leaders of Nazi Germany had set as their goal, was, in the end, created to work against them.

But those who resist must, in their turn, think of the future. The victory that was slowly approaching would not in itself satisfy them: It was necessary to know the uses to which it would be put and what the Europe of tomorrow would be like. In the clandestine journalism of the time, we sometimes find echoes of the debates that took place on this subject within various national resistance groups and movements.* If attention was concentrated first on the immediate problems of repairing war damages and of adapting national social and economic structures to new conditions, the desire was no less widespread to look beyond state frontiers and cure Europe of the disease of nationalism.

There was nothing surprising, therefore, in the convergence in 1944 of declarations from several resistance movements in favor of European federation. During the first general congress of the Combat movement, held in Algiers in March, 1944, Henry Frenay made an appeal to "all men of the European resistance." A little later, the French Committee for

* See Henri Michel and Boris Mirkine-Guetzevitch: *Les idées politiques et sociales de la Résistance en France: Documents clandestins 1940–44* (Paris, 1954), and *L'Europe de Demain* (Centre d'action pour la fédération européenne; Neuchâtel, 1945). I have also consulted my own collection of texts and manuscripts.

European Federation came out with a manifesto that affirmed that "a society of nations patterned on a league of states is doomed to failure," and that:

> Europe can develop along the lines of economic progress, democracy, and peace only if nation-states federate and hand over to a federal European state control of the economic and commercial organization of Europe, the sole right to have an army and to intervene against any attempt to re-establish authoritarian regimes, the administration of foreign relations, the administration of colonial territories that are not yet ready for independence, and the creation of a European citizenship alongside national citizenship.*

Then on September 27, 1944, the National Liberation Movement in the Lyon region, which was seeking to unite all resistance movements, published at the head of its draft program an international plan based on the thesis of the French Committee.†

The Italian resistance fighters answered the French. Some of them had succeeded, as early as 1941, in circulating their proposals in favor of European collaboration and in creating the basis for a European federalist movement—which was strengthened in May, 1943, by the founding of a clandestine newspaper, *Unità europea*. In 1944, in a letter to their French comrades, the Italian federalists affirmed the necessity to give priority to the building of a European federation over the internal reconstruction of each country. It was not a question, they said, of creating a federalist party, for it would be impossible to rally the masses around this theme. But, on the other hand, it was important to furnish the various national political parties with the international program they needed. "The old types of European foreign policy are, in fact, dead," they declared. "The political, military, and economic struc-

---

* *L'Europe de Demain,* pp. 75–78.
† Mimeographed text.

tures of each country are dislocated. We are in a new situation, one in which progressive parties, freed of the resistance once given them by now wavering diplomats, can—if they are sufficiently convinced of the necessity of European federation —realize what in the past was only a utopia."*

We find these same themes, advanced with the same ardor and optimism, in the draft declaration issued in July by members of the European resistance in Denmark, France, Italy, Norway, the Netherlands, Poland, Czechoslovakia, and Yugoslavia. (It was also signed by an anti-Nazi German resistance fighter.) These men of the resistance, who proposed a federal union with a government directly responsible to the peoples, an army dependent exclusively on it, and a supreme court, demanded that "all measures taken between the cessation of hostilities and the establishment of the peace" be taken "as a function of the demands of federal organization." They added: "They [the signatories] promise to consider their respective national problems as special aspects of the European problem as a whole."†

European resistance fighters were not alone, above and beyond their rejection of Hitler's new order, in their concern to create a federation of free states "with equal rights, capable of creating the conditions in which spiritual independence and cultural traditions would flower, and subject at the same time to the common law of reason and morality," as Thomas Mann said in a radio speech in New York in January, 1943. The governments were making projects and drawing up plans as well. Some of them even concluded agreements that we can consider the cornerstones of the new European edifice. On January 15, 1942, for instance, the governments of the kingdoms of Greece and Yugoslavia signed a treaty foreshadowing the establishment of a "Balkan Union." On January 23 of the same year, the Czech and Polish governments agreed to lay

* *L'Europe de Demain*, pp. 78–82.
† *Ibid.*, pp. 68–75.

the foundations for a "Confederation of Poland and Czecho-slovakia." These two conventions contained similar clauses concerning the establishment by the contracting parties of common programs in foreign affairs, military affairs, economic and financial affairs, social policy, and communications. More-over, the authors of the two agreements envisioned the same possibility of admitting to their confederations other states that might wish to join. "The High Contracting Parties," said Article 10 of the Greek-Yugoslav treaty, "envisage with satisfaction the future adhesion to this agreement of other Balkan states ruled by governments freely and legally consti-tuted." And on the same day that they signed their agreement, the Polish and Czech governments declared their intention to collaborate with the reconstituted Balkan Union, "expressing . . . their conviction," as they said, "that the security and prosperity of the area of Europe situated between the Baltic and Aegean Seas depend on the collaboration of [these] two confederations."*

The agreements were welcomed in England, where discus-sions on the political reconstruction of Europe were continu-ing. *The Economist*, although pleased with them, found them somewhat timid.† In its view, the security of Eastern Europe demanded still greater integration. Eden referred to this in a speech of September 26, 1942:

> Smaller states, I am glad to say, are also alive to the need of collaboration among themselves. There are Polish-Czech and Greek-Yugoslav agreements, both of which call for and express a sense of unity. We shall continue to foster such agreements and encourage smaller states to weld themselves into larger, though not exclusive, groupings. Thus they will be better able, in collaboration with the great powers, to play a part in main-taining peace.

* See *Foreign Policy Reports* (New York), March 15, 1942, and *Czecho-slovak sources and documents*, No. 2 (March, 1943): *Struggle for Freedom* (New York, Czechoslovak Information Service).
† *The Economist*, January 24, 1942, pp. 94–95.

Some months later, on March 21, 1943, Churchill took up the problem of Europe in his turn:

I hope we shall not lightly cast aside all the immense work which was accomplished by the creation of the League of Nations. Certainly we must take as our foundation the lofty conception of freedom, law and morality which was the spirit of the League. We must try—I am speaking of course only for ourselves—to make the Council of Europe, or whatever it may be called, into a really effective League, with all the strongest forces concerned woven into its texture, with a High Court to adjust disputes, and with forces, armed forces, national or international or both, held ready to impose these decisions and prevent renewed aggression and the preparation of future wars.

Anyone can see that this Council when created must eventually embrace the whole of Europe, and that all the main branches of the European family must some day be partners in it. What is to happen to the large number of small nations whose rights and interests must be safeguarded? Here let me ask what would be thought of an army that consisted only of battalions and brigades, and which never formed any of the larger and higher organizations like army corps. It would soon get mopped up. It would therefore seem, to me at any rate, worthy of patient study that side by side with the Great Powers there should be a number of groupings of States of Confederations which would express themselves through their own chosen representatives, the whole making a Council of great States and groups of States.*

It would seem that Churchill then envisioned a generalization of the formula adopted by the Greeks and the Yugoslavs, the Czechs and the Poles. A Europe of small states grouped in federations would be bounded by the two great victorious European powers, Soviet Russia and England. This concept seems to have been widely shared in government circles in England. They realized that the defeat of France and the extension of Nazi and Fascist domination over Europe made

* Winston S. Churchill, *Onwards to Victory: War Speeches, 1943* (London and Boston, 1944), pp. 36–37.

it incumbent on the Allies to reconstruct, starting from zero.

But what would remain after the defeat of Germany and Japan? A trio of powers in which Great Britain might play only a secondary role. Through her isolated resistance of 1940, she had created the conditions for final victory. But she would come out of this war impoverished, if not absolutely ruined. "There is nothing left in the till," cried Marshal Smuts in a speech at the end of 1943. What could be done to maintain Britain between the two "colossi?" An Anglo-German alliance being rejected—as was a Franco-British alliance, because of the weakness of France—there remained the community of Anglo-Saxon peoples, which would, however, put Great Britain in the position of a second-rate power and keep her in a marginal position in relation to Europe. Now, England—everyone seems to agree on this point—cannot isolate herself from Europe. She is geographically too close to allow Europe to organize politically without her. She could not now escape from this geographic constant any more than she could in previous centuries. British participation in the political restoration of Europe was absolutely necessary. Mr. E. H. Carr underlined this point and, through him, so did *The Times*.* Marshal Smuts expressed the same opinion with still greater force and with all the prestige attached to his person, in a speech that marked the beginning of a new era.

Great Britain must depend, he argued, not only on the Commonwealth and the Empire, but on all the European states, all the Western democracies, who (it had now been proved to them) were not capable of resisting the enterprises of the great powers alone and who must feel that their place is at England's side. "Their way of life is with Great Britain, their outlook and their future are with Great Britain and the next world-wide British system," said Marshal Smuts. Thus

* "Foreign Policy in Transition," *The Times* (London), November 18–20, 1943.

would be constituted a "great European state, great not only as an empire and commonwealth spreading itself out over all continents, but great as a power on this continent, associated with the other great powers on the basis of equality for the direction of nations."*

England was thus to be the catalytic agent of a federated Europe or group of European federations—not of a Europe with which she would be integrated, but one which would, rather, be attached to her world system, of which the Commonwealth and Empire were the other elements. But the success of such a plan obviously depended on the agreement of the great allies—the Soviet Union and the United States—and Russia, in particular, had interests in Europe. The organization of the Continent could not be accomplished, *The Times* thought, except within the framework of an Anglo-Russian alliance, which would have the effect of developing zones of influence. It remained to be seen where the limits of these zones of influence would be fixed; Churchill would have liked to see them pushed as far to the East as possible. But the question could only remain open since, as yet, the objectives of Stalinist policy were not clear.

The little that was known of them was not encouraging. In May, 1943, the announcement of the dissolution of the Comintern had given rise to certain illusions among Westerners who were ill informed of the workings of the Communist mind and poorly prepared to grasp the meaning of a change in tactics. These illusions were, however, progressively destroyed in the face of the marked opposition of the Soviet Government to attempts to create an East European federation. The *New Statesman* and *The Economist* had thought it possible to conclude, from the support given by the U.S.S.R. to the Moscow Declaration on Austria, that the Soviet Government would not oppose a federation of states in Eastern

* As cited in *The Times*, December 3, 1943, p. 8.

Europe. An *Izvestia* article (of November 18, 1943) replied, saying that the Soviet Union would oppose any attempt to create a "security belt," whatever the formula. Moscow considered the numerous proposals made in the West for the federation of Europe as manifestations of anti-Soviet policy. *Izvestia* noted that at the Moscow Conference, Molotov had officially stated the opposition of the U.S.S.R. to any federative organization of Eastern Europe.

The adoption of this position was accompanied by diplomatic actions designed to permit the U.S.S.R. to affirm its presence in the East: a progressive hardening and then breaking off of diplomatic relations with Poland; the signature, on December 12, 1943, of an aid-and-assistance pact with Czechoslovakia, which involved the breaking of the Polish-Czech Convention of January, 1942—and which consequently broke up the attempt to create a federation of states on Russia's border—and at the same time brought Czechoslovakia into Moscow's orbit.

Soviet opposition to the European and British plans for federation or confederation was matched by hesitation on the part of the United States. It was true that Churchill's speech had been favorably received in America because it underlined the necessity of agreement and collaboration of the three great powers, if the federative plans were to succeed; it was true that leaders of American public opinion appeared to approve of the European attempts to organize. But the editorials in *The Times* in favor of an Anglo-Russian alliance leading to British and Soviet zones of influence in Europe provoked, on the other hand, a lively and disapproving reaction in the United States, where the division of Europe or the world into zones of influence was considered as a manifestation of precisely the kind of power politics that had led to two world wars. This was the opinion held in the Department of State and by Roosevelt. The President, Coudenhove-Kalergi noted bitterly, did not want to hear talk of a European federation.*

The French position was also somewhat different from that of their British ally. They were not prepared to play a secondary role in a Europe gravitating toward the British world system. In response to Marshal Smuts's speech, there was a veritable taking-up of arms by the spokesmen for the resistance. *Combat*'s answer was a virulent article in which it affirmed its faith in the future of a united Europe.† Then General de Gaulle in his turn outlined his conception of European unity in a speech at Algiers on March 18, 1944. "It is only too clear," he said, "that what prevents equilibrium in the present politics of the camp of liberty is the absence of the greatest part of Europe." This Europe, now reduced to silence, would emerge again. De Gaulle continued: "It is then that the actions and influence, in sum, the value of France will be—in accord with the will of history, geography, and good sense—essential to Europe, as she orients herself and re-establishes her contact with the world." France must therefore prepare to play a "European role" in Europe where certain countries would group together, always with due regard to their national sovereignties. De Gaulle envisioned his country in a Western grouping "as inclusive as possible . . . established on an economic basis. . . . The English Channel, the Rhine, and the Mediterranean would be the arteries of this grouping, which would extend outward to Africa and the Orient." It would "constitute one of the most important centers in a world organization of production, trade, and security."‡

A measure of agreement seems thus to have existed among Europeans on the necessity of unifying the capacities of Euro-

* Richard N. Coudenhove-Kalergi, *J'ai choisi l'Europe* (Paris, 1952), pp. 280–81.
† No. 53, December, 1943.
‡ *Discours* (Paris: Egloff, 1945), II, 218–20.

pean nations. But this convergence of views could not mask rather extensive differences in their concepts of political collaboration and on the degree of integration. Each nation saw the reconstruction of Europe as a function of its own interests and within different geographical and historical perspectives. Some envisioned an essentially Balkan or Danubian federation to be tied to Western Europe. Others thought of a Nordic federation. For the English, the European confederation would be part of a British world system, while De Gaulle considered France as the natural center of a Western grouping. In Norway and in Belgium, the tendency was to think that the regroupment of forces should center around the Atlantic.

The situation in 1945 was such that plans and projects were pushed into the background. The war had transformed Europe into a battlefield. It had created a void in Germany, where the Allies were trying to administer a bankruptcy that was simply the result of their absurd demand for unconditional surrender. The political scene was dominated by two extra-European powers whose meeting in the heart of the Northern Plain was to play a determining role.

Now, it is evident that the perspective with which those two powers came to the Continent, of which they were each a natural extension, differed from the view of it shared by Europeans. The centers of decision in world politics had shifted to Washington and Moscow, and it was between these two capitals, between these two poles, that a close dialogue, bypassing Europe, was to be established. For both powers, it was not so much a question of the unity of Europe as of the world, for it was on a global scale that problems were to be approached and settled. The hopes of Roosevelt and other American leaders were focused on the Grand Alliance consecrated at San Francisco and on its transformation into an instrument of peace and international cooperation. In the eyes of Stalin and the leaders of the Soviet Union, the defeat of

Germany and of the fascism it incarnated was simply a step toward the victory of socialism. It was around the U.S.S.R., fatherland of the proletariat, that the nations of Europe and of the world should be regrouped. The Soviet Army advanced this type of liberation in the territories it occupied, thus setting the frontiers of its Europe prior to any negotiation with the Allies.

In these early dialogues, Europeans scarcely had an opportunity to make themselves heard. It is true that Great Britain tried to participate, but incontestable as her rights may have been—and resolved as her leaders were to have them recognized—the disproportion of forces was too marked. In any event, other tasks occupied the British people, who, in voting their great wartime leader out of office, had expressed their wish to give priority to domestic affairs. Once more, as soon as hostilities had ceased, the great mercantile democracy took refuge in internal problems, underestimating the importance of exploiting the victory. The building of socialism in England —the logical result of the transformation in social and economic structures that the war had brought about—took precedence over the great problems of world politics, which, from the standpoint of the Grand Alliance, would in any event not pose grave difficulties among the victors.

On the Continent itself, people were preoccupied by the urgent requirements of reconstruction: to feed the people; to re-establish transport systems and economic organizations destroyed by war; to restore the authority of the state, which had been ruined by defeat and occupation; to eliminate the results of the corrupting presence of a foreign power—all this in a climate of fever and passion in which public and private interests were confused, in which personal vengeance took on the appearance of justice, in which the attitudes and uncertainties of 1940 were coldly evaluated in the pitiless light of 1945. No, the European nations were too preoccupied, too scarred by the presence of death that had haunted them for years, not to wish, first and foremost, to find themselves, to reaffirm their will to live.

Events had separated the European nations one from another and created special problems that had to be resolved before they could look beyond their frontiers. Eastern Europe was struggling with its liberators. Greece was caught in the meshes of civil war. Italy was still partially in the camp of the vanquished; Germany was subject to the arbitrary will of her conquerors. Moreover, there was no longer a single Germany, but several, and no one knew what would become of them—whether they would be regrouped, where their borders would be set, how their peoples would live, who would lead them.

In this chaos, in this general confusion, in this anguish—prolonged after the cessation of hostilities by the diversity of situations and conditions—who still spoke of building a new Europe?

And yet there was still hope. The defeat of the European nations, their loss of political power, did not necessarily deprive Europe of all possibility of expansion. And thus, in the depths of despair, one question kept recurring and soon became the subject of thorough and detailed study: What is the European spirit? Is it not by this spirit that Europe is distinguished from Asia, that it is defined, circumscribed, and extended all at once? Independently of politics, Valéry wrote, Europe "has distinguished itself clearly from all other parts of the world. Not only by its policy, but in spite of this policy and rather against, Europe has developed to the extreme the freedom of its spirit; combined a passion to understand with a will for rigor; invented a precise and active curiosity; created, through an obstinate search, results which can be exactly compared and added to one another a capital of very powerful laws and procedures."*

* Paul Valéry, "Grandeur et Décadence de l'Europe," in *Regards sur le monde actuel* (Paris, 1945).

It was around this theme that the participants in the Rencontres Internationales of Geneva joined in September, 1946. If they all agreed in noting the failure and bankruptcy of European policy and in condemning the errors that had caused it, they in equal unanimity concluded not only on a hopeful note, but with a proclamation that Europe's life was not ended, that she could still play her role of guide and leader among nations, that her contribution was essential.

Let us listen to Denis de Rougemont: "Europe looks bad," he began: "She has lost the war; she is in the process of losing the post-war. . . . If there is fighting in tomorrow's Europe, it will be in the name of democracy against the people, in the name of the people against freedom . . . that is to say, in the name of one confusion against another confusion, of a superstition against a myth." And how did he conclude? "One day, it is not impossible, it is even probable . . . that the Russians, like the Americans, will come to study the secret of our disorder and of our orders—if not they, then their children." Because Europe, the "memory of the world," for this very reason does not cease "to invent . . . it will remain the point of extreme virulence of spiritual creation."

Let us give ear to Stephen Spender: "Europe seems destined for disintegration and a return to chaos." Such is his beginning. And his conclusion: "Europe is the part of the world where men are in the best position to face their situation and to change it. In Europe one finds the greatest concentration of traditions that have not become rigid, but that are still capable of adapting to modern conditions."

And Karl Jaspers, having recalled what properly belongs to Europe—liberty, history, and science—affirmed: "We Europeans, we can find encouragement in this thought, that what Europe has produced must be spiritually surpassed by Europe itself. The essence of Europe is several millennia old. This gives it the chance to be able to continue this movement, in the present world situation, with a view to new creation."

An investigation born of anguish and despair thus ended in affirmations of confidence in the future*: Europe has the resources necessary for recovery—provided that by avowing her errors, she once again recognizes her spiritual mission.

But how was this will to recover to be translated into politics? How was nationalism, unanimously condemned, to be surmounted? The idea of confederation or federation came up again. But its form remained vague, its contours poorly outlined. The affirmation of a universalist vocation, which can and should no longer be expressed in the form of political domination, singularly complicated the problem. From the moment the planners sought to pass from thought to action, the same question kept coming up: Where is Europe? Where are its frontiers to be set? On the Rhine? On the Vistula? On the Neman? At the Urals? In order to distinguish the European nations from others, would it be necessary to measure the length of time during which they had been exposed to the influence of Greece and Rome, to evaluate the depth of Christian convictions and the solidity of Biblical knowledge? Would one take refuge in a new *limes* or, conversely, proclaim that Europe is wherever men think of themselves as Europeans? Would one include Soviet Russia, where the influence of Karl Marx had been superimposed on that of Peter the Great? "European" Russia cannot be politically dissociated from the territories east of the Urals; in that case, Europe extends to the Pacific. If one excludes Russia, does one not miss a unique chance, which the war seemed to have created, to re-establish bonds broken by the Bolshevik Revolution and to benefit once again from the contribution of the great Russian people? It was necessary to safeguard the alliance of 1941, said George Lukacs at the Rencontres Internationales. Many of the other participants thought as he did, and two of the speakers who appeared to express some doubt on the possibility of Soviet

* Rencontres internationales de Genève, *L'Esprit européen* (Neuchâtel, 1947).

participation in the construction of Europe denied, when criticized, that their remarks were meant to express a preference. One would like to avoid a choice. The European federation was to be one element of a world federation, perhaps even a stage leading to it. This was exactly what most of the planners and theorizers on European federation had said during the war; their Europe was part of a global security system. In what way? They could not say. The ambiguity of the formula masked an uncertainty and did not resolve the problem at hand: Where does Europe begin? Where does it end?

In the West, the situation appeared at first glance simpler: The limits of this peninsula of the Asian continent were fixed, after all, by the sea. But what of the British Isles? What of Great Britain, center of a commonwealth spread across the seven seas, heart of an empire that, Churchill had just reminded Roosevelt, the British had not fought a war to see destroyed. None of the British policy-makers, favorable as they may have been to a grouping of European nations, wished to see Great Britain included in a European federation. Such was the conclusion of the debates of the Assembly of the Federal Union held on September 23 and 24, 1944. Such was the opinion of one of the most ardent promoters of European union, Sir Walter Layton.* Such was the opinion shared by Churchill and Labour Party leaders. Those who in their heart of hearts had hoped to see a renewal of the offer to form an indissoluble union between France and England now heard from the mouth of the British statesman himself that it was no longer feasible. Circumstances in 1945 were no longer the same.

Was it necessary to exclude from the Europe to be the England through whose agency European liberties and the hope of a better future had been recovered? A Europe without

* Sir Walter Layton, "The British Commonwealth and World Order," Sidney Ball Lecture, March 3, 1944 (London: Oxford University Press [Barnett House Papers, No. 27]).

Great Britain is singularly shrunken. It lacks space to develop its economy and to adapt its strategy to modern armaments. Let us think of June 18, 1940, of the appeal broadcast to the French: "France is not alone. She has a vast empire behind her. She can ally with the British Empire that controls the sea and is continuing the struggle." But the inclusion of England, while assuring the presence of Europe on the seven seas, at the same time complicates, not to say compromises, any strictly European political construction.

As for the United States, her situation appeared clear: An ocean separates her from Europe. But does it really? Is not European or "Western" civilization in the final analysis an Atlantic civilization? Although the United States had been built with her back turned on Europe by pioneers who pushed to the West to occupy in progression all the land up to the Pacific coast, and although Americans had been tempted to follow the advice of those political leaders who recommended abstention from European affairs, ties with the Old World had nonetheless never been broken. On the contrary, they had become closer as the seas grew narrower, so that the Atlantic world, instead of being almost exclusively under the influence of Europe, had become a center of exchanges, of diverse influences.

The Americanization of the Old World had succeeded the Europeanization of the New, and it was not limited to the European continent, but spread out to Africa as well. Twice, the United States had been compelled to engage in wars she did not desire. She had to face up to the evidence that it was impossible to withdraw from Europe, that the interpenetration of interests was too far advanced. Both times she had taken up her position in the same camp, with Great Britain and France; the United States was conscious of defending Western civilization against Hitler. When Roosevelt sought a *rapprochement* with Stalin by going over Churchill's head, it was because he hoped to re-establish the ties with traditional Russia that the Bolshevik Revolution had broken, for he thought that the Soviet leader was gradually moving away from that Revolution. But the conflicts between Roosevelt and his British ally—even the quarrel about the Empire— were of secondary importance compared to the ideological chasm that separated the great liberal capitalist democracy of North America from the Stalinist empire.

The American presence in Europe appeared so natural and necessary that some Americans thought that the Atlantic should be the center of a regroupment of forces. We have seen the development of the idea of Atlantic union alongside that of European union. The Atlantic Charter, although it was only a declaration of principles, not a treaty between two states, had given to the Atlantic idea both *éclat* and influence. Presented at the gravest moment of Great Britain's lone struggle against Hitler, it had attested to the real and profound solidarity of the two English-speaking peoples. The United States had not yet become directly involved in the war, but her President had not hesitated to say publicly what camp the country was in, and why. An agreement on principles, but also a coincidence of interests. The British resistance served the interests of the United States. It gave the United States the time needed to mobilize, after a long period of self-imposed blindness to the danger of Hitler's rise. England—of which it had been said between the wars that she would fight down to the last Frenchman—was now fighting for the Americans and for the defense of the free world.

Roosevelt, however, was prudent. He knew the American political milieu well enough to realize that he had to allow time for Americans to become conscious of the danger threatening the country. Others, less burdened by the responsibilities of power, were less reserved. Wendell Willkie, his unlucky rival, had already proposed "an economic and social union of the United States and the British Commonwealth," and had thus come to share the views of the group of men who had encouraged Churchill to propose a Franco-British union. Moreover, the two proposals had a common origin. They were inspired by Clarence Streit's *Union Now* (published in the spring of 1939 and translated into French under the title *Union ou Chaos*, which better reflects its prophetic accents), an eloquent appeal for Atlantic union. Streit had followed the career of the League of Nations in Geneva and had noted its failures. For him, there was no other solution, if one wished to avoid chaos, but the establishment of a federative tie between the United States on the one hand, and the British Commonwealth and the European states of the Atlantic coast on the other. What was necessary was "a union now of the democracies that the North Atlantic and a thousand other things already unite, the union of these few peoples in a great federal republic built on and for the thing they share most, their common democratic principle of government for the sake of individual freedom." The work was a resounding success and gave rise to many and diverse reactions. It is not surprising that the creation of an Atlantic union was seen by numerous authors not only as a possibility but as a necessity.

The discussion continued throughout the war. Walter Lippmann devoted a chapter of his book *U.S. Foreign Policy* to the "Atlantic Community" that was to constitute the basis of a new American security system. Without recommending an integration as complete as that proposed by Streit, he underlined the coincidence of interests existing between the nations of Western Europe and the North American continent. "Not what men say, not what they think they feel," he remarked in conclusion, "but what in fact when they have to act they actually do—that is the test of community. By that test there is a great community on this earth from which no member can be excluded and none can resign. This community had its geographical center in the great basin of the Atlantic."

Certain British voices echoed the Americans. The activity

of the Federal Union in Great Britain, which was very intensive just before and during the first years of the war, slowed down somewhat, it is true, because of the increasing demands made by the war itself. But some of its members nevertheless continued their studies. If they leaned in the direction of a world federation, they did not give up the idea of regional groupings or associations of states. Among other solutions, they thought of a union between the English-speaking peoples. Their report in the spring of 1942, having analyzed the evolution of the military collaboration between the United States and Great Britain, concluded in these terms:

All these developments constitute progress toward the unification of the defense system of the English-speaking peoples, with a single air force, united navies, and a single banking, monetary, customs, economic planning and transport system. The common expenses of the two countries in the field of economic reconstruction (they would be the producers, buyers, depositories, transporters and distributors of essential foodstuffs and raw materials) as well as the realization of the economic clauses of the Atlantic Charter are aimed in the same direction. But so high a degree of military and economic association can be maintained in the long run only on the basis of a common governmental mechanism. The identity of language and the similarity of institutions and political tradition among the members of the British Commonwealth make the creation of such a mechanism technically possible. The growing tendency to consider proposals for a common "citizenship" and even for a union, coming from both sides of the Atlantic, proves that the establishment of such a mechanism has already penetrated into the sphere of things that are psychologically possible.*

On the Continent, advocates of Atlantic union were no doubt less numerous. They were recruited especially in countries like Norway and Belgium, which traditionally had been oriented to the Atlantic world and which feared being enclosed in a strictly European political organization. The his-

---

* *L'Europe de Demain*, pp. 170–71.

torian Jacques Pirenne became the most ardent defender of the Atlantic thesis. In his *Grands Courants de L'Histoire Universelle*, he had already emphasized the basic contrast between the agrarian society of Central Europe and Russia—a stronghold of feudalism and autocracy—and the Western economic system, where easier communication, thanks to abundant watercourses, had favored the development of commerce and thus of a bourgeois society. In the analysis of the new world balance to which he proceeded in 1944, he was naturally led to an emphasis of the overlapping interests and the likenesses of economic and social structures in the Atlantic nations. "The present war will not have been fought in vain," he wrote, "if the statesmen in whose hands the fate of the Western countries lies make themselves the instruments of the historical evolution of their peoples and crown the war effort by uniting them into a great Atlantic federation."*

European federation, Atlantic community, world unity! These themes, each of which had its supporters, were not necessarily mutually exclusive. On the contrary, everyone agreed that modern scientific and technical progress, and the resultant development of all kinds of exchanges, made necessary—especially at the end of a disastrous war and with the universal memory of the Hiroshima explosion—an advanced coordination of international affairs, even the very integration of independent states into continental or intercontinental ensembles that would, perhaps, collaborate. But more and more, circumstances were to impose a choice.

* See Jacques Pirenne and Jacques-Henri Pirenne, *La Belgique devant le nouvel équilibre du monde* (Neuchâtel, 1944).

⑂ [2] ⑄

First Efforts

Those who wish to understand the climate that nurtured the Grand Alliance should reread the declarations of its leaders. At the end of the Tehran Conference, Roosevelt, Churchill, and Stalin said:

> We are sure that our concord will make it an enduring peace. We recognize fully the supreme responsibility resting upon us and all the United Nations, to make a peace which will command the good will of the overwhelming mass of the peoples of the world, and banish the scourge and terror of war for many generations.
>
> With our diplomatic advisers, we have surveyed the problems of the future. We shall seek the cooperation and the active participation of all nations, large and small, whose peoples in heart and mind are dedicated, as are our own peoples, to the elimination of tyranny and slavery, oppression and intolerance. We will welcome them, as they may choose to come, into a world family of democratic nations.*

* *Foreign Relations of the United States: Diplomatic Papers: The Conferences at Cairo and Tehran, 1943* (Washington: U.S. Government Printing Office, 1961), p. 641.

The tone is paternal. It is a perfect expression of what could be called the style of that coalition. Leaders of governments and armies have addressed their peoples and their soldiers in every war. They have usually employed a thunderous and vivid style, seeking striking formulas to express the vision of what lay at the end, after the sacrifices they had still to ask —of enrichment or liberty, of the victory of law, justice, or democracy. Here all the promises had already been made, and neither Roosevelt nor Churchill could offer more than what others before them had promised. But the language they used differed from that of their predecessors. There was nothing inflammatory or sonorous about it. They addressed themselves to the common man as to a child whose attentive parents take good care of him. They spoke of a great "world family of democratic nations," and they spoke of it in the "fireside" style that the President of the United States knew how to use so successfully. In fact, the style of the Grand Alliance was Roosevelt's.

This style characterized not only the official documents. It can be found in speeches, in private correspondence, and in the press. It was the expression of the aspirations and convictions of public opinion:

> We really believed in our hearts that this was the dawn of the new day we had all been praying for and talking about for so many years. We were absolutely certain that we had won the first great victory of the peace—and by "we" I mean *all* of us, the whole civilized human race. The Russians had proved that they could be reasonable and far-seeing and there wasn't any doubt in the minds of the President or any of us that we could live with them peacefully for as far into the future as any of us could imagine.*

This text is often cited because it is characteristic of the state of mind of the men who formulated United States

* Harry Hopkins, in Robert E. Sherwood, *Roosevelt and Hopkins: An Intimate History* (New York: Harper & Brothers, 1950).

foreign policy. But one could cite many others from Europe as well as America that express the same sentiment: The one way to end wars once and for all is by establishing a world system of security. Popular sentiment supported the establishment of the United Nations, and even those who had criticisms or doubts about its structure recognized the absolute necessity for its creation.

But if the theme of world unity had endless variations, and if there was unanimity in recognizing the necessity for an international world organization of all peoples, it did not follow that agreement existed on the definition and interpretation of the terms used. Discussion among the Allies, difficult enough during the war, revealed a basic divergence of interests as soon as the hostilities had ceased. The myth of world unity lost both its persuasion and unifying power in the light of the facts. Stalin reminded everyone of the limits of inter-Allied collaboration by referring to the Leninist theory of imperialism in his speech of February 9, 1949: There cannot be real peace so long as capitalism exists, for it creates imperialism, which inevitably leads to war.

For those who would not pay attention to this declaration, the hardening of Soviet demands was proved by Molotov's attitude at the various conferences of foreign ministers. Little by little, Eastern Europe was closed off from the West to undergo a *Gleichschaltung* that was pursued pitilessly in 1946 and 1947. One by one, men whose political careers had been marked by Western influences were eliminated to be replaced by new ruling groups trained or claiming to have been trained in Marxist-Leninist thought and methods. This cleansing operation continued despite the protests of the English and American governments, who, given the map of Europe as it was at the end of the war, had to accept the Soviet Union's interpretation of the Yalta Agreements.

In Germany, the equivocations of the Potsdam Agreements were equally apparent. Germany's division into zones of occupation had not been balanced by the establishment of a central administration or interzonal economic exchange. Each of the Allies barricaded himself in his zone, which he administered according to his own methods. Measures of "denazification" and democratization, although harsh everywhere, were applied in different ways. Quarrels arose over reparations and the dismantling of industrial installations, all the more serious as Western authorities realized the impasse to which strict application of measures to limit iron production would lead. How could the population of the Western occupation zones live on a soil whose agricultural yield was insufficient and absorb the huge numbers of refugees from the East if forbidden to exploit its industrial potential? The absurdity of the policy (in which one can discern shadows of the celebrated Morgenthau Plan) was evident to everyone. Consequently, the Western Allies, who could not get the Soviets to agree to economic unification, had to organize among themselves and regroup their zones, thus underlining the division of Germany.

Difficulties were no less great for the Western victors. In France, national unity, which apparently had been renewed during the Resistance and had found expression in the association of the three great parties—Communist, Socialist, and MRP—did not long withstand the trial of power. Once the crisis of liberation was past—a crisis at once both awesome and odious, during which the abuses of *résistancialisme* destroyed the desire for national reconciliation and weakened the hope that the arrival of new men, toughened but not tarnished by the conquest of power, had created—it became necessary to recognize certain fundamental disagreements in political concepts and methods. Very early, too early, General de Gaulle, who had personified the Resistance will for unity during the war, had withdrawn, so as to avoid a choice he refused to make but to which circumstances seemed to force him, between personal dictatorship and a dictatorship of the parties. A tripartite coalition survived his departure by more than a year, until the beginning of May, 1947. But during this period, while attention was focused on constitutional problems, the tension between the Communist Party and its Socialist and MRP associates continued to grow, encouraging instability because of the impossibility of making any either economic or political decisions. Italy, which had reversed her course in time and found men to represent her who were acceptable to the Allies, managed to escape occupation, and, at the beginning of 1947, obtained a not unfavorable treaty. But she had not been spared by the war: The slow retreat of the German armies along the peninsula and the brief spasm of the Republican Fascist Party had caused much destruction; the country was poor; the Mussolini adventure had cost it dear. The postwar years were difficult. The economic and financial problems of reconstruction of this country without great natural resources were compounded by the problems that inevitably arise with a change of regime: A democratic republic succeeded both monarchy and fascism. Happily for Italy, the young republic was to have at its disposal a group of new political leaders, tried and true patriots of real intellectual worth whom exile had protected and matured. And the presence of the Vatican and the action of the clergy were to exercise a stabilizing influence. But the existence of a powerful Communist Party, organized like a state within a state, was a heavy burden that intensified the tension during the difficult period of reconstruction.

Thus the breaking-up of the Grand Alliance and the consequent division of the world into two camps not only transformed the line drawn across Europe by the armies at the end of the war into a permanent frontier; it also inhibited the growth of national unity and weakened the two states that were then the bastions of the West on the Continent. Simultaneously, the growing pressure that the U.S.S.R. exercised on certain West European and Mediterranean countries via its Balkan associates or the action of Communist parties—a pressure all the more tangible as Europe was living on the edge of economic collapse—made clear the danger of Soviet seizure of the whole Continent. Greece, subjected to the combined action of internal and external Communist forces, was not capable of resisting by its own means. Turkey, faced once again with the Soviet demand for participation in the control of the Straits, had, for the sake of prudence, to keep large numbers of men under arms.

This deterioration of the situation within the allied camp, the meaning and real causes of which were not immediately clear to governments or the public, elicited two reactions in Europe and the United States. In Western Europe, it encouraged a regroupment of forces and an intensification of the efforts to organize politically that part of the Continent still free of Soviet domination. The Soviet Government, by reaffirming its belief in the ultimate victory of socialism and by its attempt to provoke revolutionary outbreaks wherever it could, did more than destroy the myth of world unity: It fixed the frontier of Europe, which all the discussions during the war had not been able to do and, at the same time, forced the Europeans to abandon theory for action, or else face extinction. But the Europeans were not the only ones concerned. American policy was subjected to re-examination; as a result the United States halted the process of disengagement from the positions held at the end of the war and reaffirmed its presence in Europe and the Mediterranean.

Once more, it was Winston Churchill who sounded the alarm by saying what others, tied down by the immediate responsibilities of power, thought they could not say so clearly. His speech at Fulton, Missouri, on March 5, 1946, which the Soviets immediately attacked as a provocation and which the Labour Government immediately disclaimed, was, in fact, only a description of an acknowledged situation: "From

Stettin in the Baltic to Trieste in the Adriatic, an iron curtain has descended across the continent. Behind that line lie all the capitals of the ancient states of Central and Eastern Europe." There, Communist parties, although reduced in membership, had seized power; police states had been developed; except in Czechoslovakia, it was no longer possible to speak of democracy. Churchill reviewed the situation on the borders of Soviet Russia, noted the apprehension of Turkey and Iran, Communist pressure in the Soviet occupation zone, continued agitation in France and Italy. "Except in the British Commonwealth and in the United States, where Communism is in its infancy, the Communist parties or fifth columns constitute a growing challenge and peril to Christian civilization." It was not that the Soviet Union wanted war; what she wanted were the fruits of war. But, the Russians respect force. Hence the necessity of a firm policy of unified forces—European forces, and those of the two great English-speaking nations:

> If the population of the English-speaking commonwealths be added to that of the United States with all that such co-operation implies in the air, on the sea, all over the globe and in science and in industry, and in moral force, there will be no quivering, precarious balance of power to offer its temptation to ambition or adventure.

A few months later, in his famous Zurich speech of September 19, 1946, Churchill addressed himself directly to the Europeans, speaking to them of the "tragedy of Europe." There was, he argued, a remedy to the accumulated misery and disorders of the war: It was to reconstitute the European family, to build a United States of Europe, beginning with a close association between France and Germany:

> The first step in the re-creation of the European family must be a partnership between France and Germany. In this way only can France recover the moral leadership of Europe. There can be no revival of Europe without a spiritually great France and a spiritually great Germany.

This speech had considerable impact. The war had ended only a little more than a year before and its effects were still felt everywhere. Germany, in this month of September, 1946, was simply an occupied territory and it was impossible to know how or when it would cease to be a mere object of international politics. Yet Churchill affirmed that there was no salvation for Europe except in a reconciliation of the two great peoples that war and Nazi tyranny had set against each other, condemned, as many thought, never to understand one another. He was not the first to point the way to reconciliation. Immediately after the war, had not General de Gaulle spoken to the Germans "in the language of Europe"? In the climate prevailing then, his remark found no echoes, nor did his speech at Bar-le-Duc in July, 1946. Churchill, on the other hand, now at the height of his glory, addressed himself to a public that was disillusioned, disturbed, and, therefore, receptive. In the gray mist of the postwar years, a period marked by material worries and by abstruse, sterile diplomatic discussions, he offered Europe more than a political solution or a popular cause. He offered hope.

From that time on, not so much because of Churchill's initiative as because of a change in the political climate, activities multiplied. All the intellectual preparations made in the shadow of war and during the early postwar months suddenly bore fruit. Projects were concretized. European militants found political leaders to talk to.

In May, 1946, Joseph Retinger, who, as adviser to General Sikorski, had been one of the most vigorous proponents of the Polish-Czech *rapprochement* and of the regroupment of the East European states,* had founded, with Paul van Zeeland, the Independent League for European Economic Cooperation, which, in 1948, became the European League for Economic

---

* Retinger's important role in the reconstruction of Europe is described in "Hommage à un grand Européen, Joseph H. Retinger," in the *Bulletin* of the Centre Européen de la Culture (Geneva), 1960–61, No. 5.

Cooperation. The League soon had branches in Belgium, Holland, Luxembourg, France, Italy, the United Kingdom, and the United States. Michel Debré, Giscard d'Estaing, and Daniel Serruy were members, as were Sir Harold Butler, Harold Macmillan, Peter Thorneycroft, Averell Harriman, and Adolf Berle.

In England, where Churchill, continuing his efforts, once again won over public opinion with his great speech at the Albert Hall on May 14, 1947, the United Europe Movement was created under his presidency. In France, the efforts of a few men (including René Courtin) culminated in June, 1947, in the formation of a French Council for United Europe, under the presidency of Raoul Dautry, with André Siegfried, Paul Bastid, Paul Ramadier, Paul Reynaud, and Pierre-Henri Teitgen as vice presidents. Some months earlier, in March, the constitution of the Nouvelles Equipes Internationales laid the basis for coordinating the policies of the Christian Democratic parties on a European scale. At the same time, a number of socialists grouped together in an International Committee for the Socialist United States of Europe, whose aims were to keep the movement for European federation from being captured by "reactionaries" and to promote a truly "socialist" United States of Europe.

Coudenhove-Kalergi had not remained inactive during this period, but had given encouragement to others, goading them into action, and had himself taken the initiative in forming a European Parliamentary Union, which held its first congress at Gstaad in September, 1947. Two hundred members from ten European legislatures participated and gave their approval to a campaign for European union. The maneuver was as ingenious as it was simple: By mobilizing these representatives, a more direct contact was established with the public, with the sovereign peoples who, one assumes, help to shape the policies of their governments. "The European Parliamentary Congress," said the resolution of Gstaad, "appeals to all the

Parliaments of Europe to use their power and influence on governments and peoples."

A parallel regroupment of forces was taking place among the federalists. At the end of 1946, after several meetings—particularly those at Hertenstein, Luxembourg, and Basel—the decision was made in Paris to create a European Union of Federalists. The Union's first congress, held at Montreux, August 27–31, 1947, had a tremendous *éclat*. The number of delegates was in itself impressive, but even more so was the serious and high quality of the reports given and work accomplished. The European Union of Federalists, which did not accept individual members but only corporate entities, did not try to compete with other groups being formed at the same time. It aspired to be a coordinating element and clearinghouse for the diffusion of federalist doctrines. Its strength was that it depended less on great political leaders than on militant believers who would dedicate themselves almost exclusively to the European cause. The definition of federalism agreed on at Montreux was, moreover, one upon which there could be general agreement:

> To federate Europe is not to "set it in order" according to a geometric plan arranged on a center or axis, but it is simply to confront, conjoin, and coordinate . . . the concrete and heterogeneous realities that are the nations, economic systems, and political traditions of Europe. And to organize them according to their particular characteristics is, at the same time, to protect and transform them.

Federalism thus permitted both unity and diversity. It sought to rise above opposition, surmount division, ignore frontiers, and join the aspirations of one and all in a single movement. The proposed European federation was already in the process of being built. It was necessary to accelerate this movement and to orient it toward the creation of a supranational European organization which, without separating

Europe from the rest of the world, would consist of a federal authority including:

1. A government responsible to individuals and groups and not to the federated states.

2. A supreme court capable of settling differences that might arise between member states of the federation.

3. An armed police force, under the command of the Federal government, whose duty would be to enforce federal decisions, without prejudice to a world security organization.*

As for the Americans, they very clearly encouraged the effort toward European unification. Churchill, in his Zurich speech, made reference to President Truman's declaration in favor of European unity. John Foster Dulles, the great foreign-policy expert of the Republican Party, publicly voiced the same views. In Congressional circles as well as in the Administration, there was an awareness of the need to stop Europe's descent toward anarchy and to put an end to Soviet encroachments. Thus, the first decision was made in 1946 to give Great Britain a loan—its purpose clearly being the prevention of economic breakdown of one of the pillars of Atlantic defense. Then, on March 12, 1947, came the proclamation of the Truman Doctrine, in which the President promised that America would "support free people who are resisting attempted subjugation by armed minorities or by outside pressures."† In deciding to give its support to Greece and Turkey, both subjected since the end of the war to increasing and threatening pressure from the Soviet world, the Government of the United States wished to underline the fact that it considered its security threatened by Soviet expansion to the eastern borders of Europe. Its affirmation of solidarity extended across the At-

* See European Union of Federalists, *Report of the First Annual Congress*, August 27–31, 1947. The report also insisted that "true democracy must express solidarity, from the base to the pinnacle, and must be harmoniously organized at all levels."

† *A Decade of American Foreign Policy, Basic Documents, 1941–49* (Washington: U. S. Government Printing Office, 1950), p. 1256.

lantic and the Mediterranean to the coasts of the Aegean Sea and Asia Minor.

It was not that the United States wished to tie herself to Europe or that she expected to create a special form of association. If she acted thus, it was because, as a world power, she could not tolerate the expansion of the sphere of influence of a power that had now become a dangerous rival, an expansion that would lead to modification of the power balance in favor of that rival. But by doing this, the United States had inextricably involved herself. If one wished to defend the lines of communications, aid to Greece and Turkey inevitably implied aid to Italy and Western Europe, both of which were also gravely threatened. From the Truman Doctrine to the Marshall Plan—first expressed in General Marshall's celebrated speech at Harvard in June, 1947—the connection is evident.

But in the interval, a policy was elaborated, objectives were decided upon. The economic aid the United States was ready to give would contribute to European integration. The United States of Europe—such was the image the American Government and people hoped for after a few years of economic cooperation. The foreign-aid act of 1948, voted by Congress after involved diplomatic negotiations and long debates, in unequivocal terms expressed the objectives of American foreign policy with regard to Europe:

SECTION 102 (a) Recognizing the intimate economic and other relationships between the United States and the nations of Europe, and recognizing that disruption following in the wake of war is not contained by national frontiers, the Congress finds that the existing situation in Europe endangers the establishment of a lasting peace, the general welfare and national interest of the United States, and the attainment of the objectives of the United Nations. The restoration or maintenance in European countries of principles of individual liberty, free institutions, and genuine independence rests largely upon the establishment of sound economic conditions, stable international economic relationships, and the achievement by the countries of Europe of a healthy economy independent of extraordinary outside assistance. The accomplishment of these objectives calls for a plan of European recovery, open to all such nations which cooperate in such plan, based on a strong production effort, the expansion of foreign trade, the creation and maintenance of internal financial stability, and the development of economic cooperation, including all possible steps to establish and maintain equitable rates of exchange and to bring about the progressive elimination of trade barriers. Mindful of the advantages which the United States has enjoyed through the existence of a large domestic market with no internal trade barriers, and believing that similar advantages can accrue to the countries of Europe, it is declared to be the policy of the United States to encourage these countries through a joint organization to exert sustained common efforts as set forth in the report of the committee of European Economic Cooperation signed at Paris on September 22, 1947, which will speedily achieve that economic cooperation in Europe which is essential for lasting peace and prosperity. It is further declared to be the policy of the people of the United States to sustain and strengthen principles of individual liberty, free institutions, and genuine independence in Europe through assistance to those countries of Europe which participate in a joint recovery program based upon self-help and mutual cooperation:

Provided, That no assistance to the participating countries herein contemplated shall seriously impair the economic stability of the United States. It is further declared to be the policy of the United States that continuity of assistance provided by the United States should, at all times, be dependent upon continuity of cooperation among countries participating in the program.

(b) It is the purpose of this title to effectuate the policy set forth in subsection (a) of this section by furnishing material and financial assistance to the participating countries in such a manner as to aid them, through their individual and concerted efforts, to become independent of extraordinary outside economic assistance within the period of operations under this title, by:

(1) promoting industrial and agricultural production in the participating countries;

(2) furthering the restoration of maintenance of the soundness of European currencies, budgets, and finances; and

(3) facilitating and stimulating the growth of international trade of participating countries with one another and with other countries by appropriate measures including reduction of barriers which may hamper such trade.*

Thus encouraged on all sides, spurred on by the Soviet menace, stimulated by the support of the United States and Great Britain, swept forward by a movement uniting intellectuals and politicians, Europe seemed finally to acquire self-awareness—she seemed finally to be trying to organize herself. The grandeur of her past and the recent catastrophe were also incitements to action. From all sides came appeals asking Europeans to organize among themselves. Caught between two great continental empires, the European peoples would recover their independence and their influence only if they united their efforts and if the states consented to real sacrifices of sovereignty. Divided, Europe was lost; united, it was a great power.

Such were the declarations repeated almost obsessively on all sides. The theme of European union advocated by various groups, developed later at the Hague "Congress of Europe," taken up by the government ministers assembled at the Paris Conference, seemed to exercise so great and growing an influence over public opinion that responsible men in public life undertook to *"bousculer leurs gouvernements,"* in the words of Paul-Henri Spaak.

In this striving toward self-awareness, Europe was forced to define herself—if only by contrast with other areas. Molotov's refusal of America's offer of economic cooperation was profoundly disappointing especially when compounded with the nonparticipation of all of Eastern Europe and with the withdrawal of Czechoslovakia. A way was nonetheless sought

* *Ibid.,* p. 1299.

to keep the door open to Eastern Europe. The participants in the Montreux Congress of the European Union of Federalists had been careful to note that the European federation they hoped to create was not directed against Soviet Russia, that it did not imply a withdrawal of the Europeans into the western part of the peninsula, that no decision would be made without "taking account of the aspirations of Eastern Europe." The division was nonetheless evident, and it was widened by the vigorous denunciation of Soviet totalitarianism made by some supporters of European federalism. Moreover, the Soviet Government's opposition to the Marshall Plan was not limited to declarations of principle: It was manifested in virtually insurrectionary strikes in Italy and France during the winter of 1947–48, and, in a still more spectacular manner, by the *coup d'état* in Prague in the spring of 1948 that brought the Communist Party to sole power in Czechoslovakia.

But the sense of their own weakness shared by so many Europeans made them distrust their American protector as much as they did the revolutionary imperialism of the U.S.S.R. They were inclined to see in both the one and the other—despite the difference in attitudes and methods—a potential conqueror. The renewed charges by the Soviet Union and European Communists that the Marshall Plan was a characteristic expression of capitalist imperialism troubled the situation still more. Attacked as American lackies, the men who had at first accepted the idea of the Marshall Plan in order to affirm their independence were forced to underline that which separated Europe from the United States, to fix the frontiers on the west as well as on the east.

Europe thus took up her position vis-à-vis the two great giants, setting them back to back against one another. The themes of the 1930's took on a new significance: Between Soviet Communism and American capitalism, Europe—the home of personalism, land made to the measure of man, heiress to Greco-Roman civilization, refuge of particularisms, meeting place of the most diverse influences—was still capable of raising her beacon and of bringing valid solutions to a world imprisoned in false dilemmas.

On the other hand, equivocation on the subject of Great Britain still persisted. Would she be associated with Europe? Or would she remain on the "outside"? Even the most "European" of the English seemed to opt for the second possibility. Churchill had concluded his Zurich speech by declaring that Great Britain and the Commonwealth, together with the United States and the Soviet Union, ought to be the friend and sponsor of the new Europe. His remark made clear that he did not include Great Britain in the European union, and this conclusion reflected the views of many others in British politics. Great Britain should base her security—this was the opinion of the Labour leaders as well as of the Conservatives—first and foremost on the Charter of the United Nations. It was also necessary to preserve both the special fraternity of the two English-speaking nations and Britain's relation with the Commonwealth, while at the same time reinforcing the ties of Europe.

But by associating too closely with European federation, Britain would risk cutting herself off from the Commonwealth and from the United States, thereby losing the freedom of movement that was one of the factors upon which her influence depended.* She was certainly ready—especially since the Soviet Union obstructed the proper functioning of the United Nations—to conclude agreements with certain neighboring states on the European continent. The Soviet menace, which caused her to sign the Treaty of Dunkirk with France in 1947, also led her to put her signature to the Brussels Treaty at the beginning of 1948. But these were only alliances of the old,

---

* See the publications of the Royal Institute of International Affairs, which reveal a great deal about the orientation of public opinion on these points, especially *France and Britain* (London, 1945), and *British Security* (London, 1946).

classic type; they did not signify that England was ready to participate in a European federation. Bevin, in a speech in the House of Commons on January 22, 1948, emphasized the necessity of consolidating Western Europe and even noted that Great Britain could not remain outside of Europe. But he made it clear that he would not propose "a formal political union with France," that he was satisfied rather to "maintain the closest possible contact and work for ever closer unity between the two nations."

It was difficult, however, to keep the distance and relative freedom of action that British leaders wanted. England's weakness as well as her geographical position, tied her fate to that of Western Europe; the United Kingdom profited as much as other European states from Marshall aid. She was thus associated in an enterprise that, above and beyond the restitution of the finances and economies of the individual nations, aimed at political integration. And there were many influential Englishmen who were members of European movements. In December, 1947, the United Europe Movement, over which Winston Churchill presided, joined—in an International Committee of the Movements for European Unity—with the European Union of Federalists, the French Council for a United Europe, and the Economic League for European Cooperation. On that Committee, Duncan Sandys collaborated actively with Joseph Retinger to prepare for the Hague Congress of Europe, and here Churchill made an almost royal entrance, acclaimed by all the participants as the spiritual father of the New Europe.

The English, who had considered the reconciliation and subsequent collaboration of France and Germany as the first step in the political reconstruction of Europe, now paradoxically found themselves occupying a central position and thus involved directly and from the very first in the European enterprise. The few Germans (including Konrad Adenauer) who were at the Hague could play only a subsidiary role: Germany was still occupied.

It was therefore between the English and the Continentals that the dialogue that dominated the Congress of Europe took place. "Make haste slowly," said Harold Macmillan to Paul Reynaud, who replied that such a proverb was hardly appropriate "for a drowning man, for a Europe faced with the dilemma of whether to unite or perish." In his keynote address, Churchill also advised moderation. He recognized that Marshall aid in the economic sphere and the joint organization of military defense would necessarily lead to closer political union. But that would not necessarily involve a sacrifice of national sovereignty. What he envisioned rather was "the gradual assumption by all the nations concerned of that larger sovereignty which can alone protect their diverse and distinctive customs and characteristics and their national traditions."* The task of the Congress of Europe was therefore to make the voice of Europe heard, so as to encourage governments to coordinate their action, and to decide on the constitution of an assembly that would represent concerted European opinion. Only at a later stage would it be possible for the governments to think of creating a European constitution.

But this prudence did not suit the West Europeans. The circumstances demanded more revolutionary decisions. "Nothing will be done," said Henri Brugmans, "so long as the dogma of sacrosanct national sovereignty is not overturned." And the European federalists were not satisfied with this mere declaration of war against nationalism; they had definite views on what the future European federation should be. They saw it "embodied" in a number of organizations: a European general staff, a European railway system, an independent administration for European coal production, a centralized organization for the development of electric power, and "a European clear-

* Winston S. Churchill, "Europe Unite," in *Europe Unite: Speeches, 1947–48* (London: Cassel & Company, 1950), p. 312.

ing house for labor supply and wages"; in addition, there would be a European government and parliament elected by "European citizens" to coordinate the action of these agencies and the many other agencies still to be created.

This debate—in which the admirable was mixed with the grotesque, as in the debates a century earlier at Frankfurt—had the advantage of forcing the partisans of a united Europe to define their position: on the one hand, there were the "unionists" (including the majority of the English), who envisioned a progressive collaboration between European states, developing as the needs and circumstances required; on the other, the federalists. But the federalists were themselves divided. There were the so-called "international" federalists, who, as Olivier Philip noted, wanted to go beyond national sovereignties but stop short of total and absolute unity, which they thought would be as dangerous as disunion; and there were the so-called "integral" federalists, who thought that the new European structure should preserve "the national, professional, and spiritual communities that are the infrastructure of national collectivities."*

They ended up by agreeing on certain recommendations. Once Reynaud's rather surprising proposal for the election of a European Constituent Assembly by universal suffrage (one deputy per one million inhabitants) had been rejected, agreement was reached on the necessity of a European assembly based on the national parliaments. And everyone acknowledged that the European federation should be open to all democratic countries, including Germany; its creation implied the merging by member states of "certain of their sovereign rights." Lastly, the cultural commission concluded by demanding a European Charter of the Rights of Man, adherence to which would be guaranteed by a European Supreme Court. It also recommended the creation of a European Cultural

* Olivier Philip, *Le problème de l'Union européenne* (Neuchâtel, 1950), p. 205.

Center independent of government control, which would "promote a sense of European community," and more particularly, facilitate intellectual and artistic exchanges and encourage the coordination of research and academic collaboration.

At the same time, another debate on fundamental principles was taking place in the economic commission, setting liberal economists against the representatives of the socialist and syndicalist schools. Agreement was hardly possible among them on issues of a technical nature, much less on affirmative programs for action. Thus, the accord was limited to general and rather negative formulas, denouncing economic nationalism, supporting the abolition of obstacles to trade and the reduction of tariffs, etc., in order to open the way to complete economic integration.

The total results may appear slight. But the Hague Congress nonetheless marked a step toward the building of the new Europe. It was, first of all, the culmination of a movement, consecrating the heretofore disparate and uncoordinated efforts of the European militants. It was a major event for everyone who participated in it; from then on, the creation of Europe was to be taken seriously. The number and quality of the participants, their importance both in European affairs and in the politics of their own countries, contributed to the growing influence of this spectacular demonstration. The continent, once apparently condemned, seemed to come to life again. That Europe still had intellectual resources and men capable of original ideas could not now be denied after these discussions in which some of Europe's most brilliant minds had confronted one another.

"True culture is not an ornament, a mere luxury, or an ensemble of unique refinements that do not concern the man on the street," said the cultural report of the Hague Congress. "It is born of a growing awareness of life, of the perpetual need to deepen the meaning of existence and to increase the power of man over things."* It was now a matter of knowing how to communicate this to the man in the street and, with him or through him, to the governments. It would not be easy, the more so since the "Europeans" did not agree on the methods to be employed.

* See Denis de Rougemont, *L'Europe en jeu* (Neuchâtel, 1948), p. 151.

{ 3 }

From European Unity to the Atlantic Pact

At the conclusion of a biography of Joseph Retinger, its author said that Retinger was "the typical man of action, who combined the qualities that were indispensable to allow him to pass unnoticed before the eyes of future historians." He warned chroniclers "against such a grave omission; it would distort any account of the real forces that shaped our world."*

It is always difficult to give a faithful and exact account of such motive forces—omissions are almost inevitable. But it is certain that a historian of contemporary Europe would commit a grievous error of judgment if he limited himself to tracing governmental acts, if he were satisfied with the study of treaties and diplomatic negotiations and of the parliamentary debates they provoke. The more one studies this period, the more one is struck by the importance of certain men—men like Joseph Retinger or, in his way, Jean Monnet—who worked outside the framework of government offices, parliaments, administrations, or interest groups. It was these men, more or less well known, who labored tirelessly, who tied together

* See "Hommage à un grand Européen," p. 50.

broken threads, established contacts, sought the right formula to end an impasse or effect a compromise. It is they who kept the idea of European federation alive, who managed to impress it upon the public mind, among the most diverse groups, and who thereby created a propitious climate for the resolutions they called for. By widening their influence and their connections, and thus by giving them direct access to politicians, the Hague Congress of Europe had opened up new possibilities of action. They could now go to work.

The first thing they did was to tighten up the coordination among Europeans divided and dispersed in different and sometimes rival groupings. The negotiations undertaken toward this goal led, on October 25, 1948, to the transformation of the International Committee for the Movements for European Unity (which united four existing organizations) into the European Movement, also including in it the Socialist Movement for the United States of Europe (the successor to the International Committee for the Socialist United States of Europe). These changes of name may appear to be of secondary importance. But the European Movement, under the honorary presidencies of Léon Blum, Winston Churchill, Alcide de Gasperi, and Paul-Henri Spaak (with Duncan Sandys as President of the Executive Council and Joseph Retinger as General Secretary), fully intended to assume complete control of operations: Its creation implied a real concentration of forces. As for the socialists, they recognized that they could not demand as a first condition of their participation the promise that a United Europe would be socialist. They satisfied themselves with the demand that the "political system to be" would not inherently exclude the possibility of socialism established through democratic means.

The basic tasks the European Movement set itself were to study the political, economic, and technical problems posed by the integration of Europe, and to inform and mobilize public opinion to encourage governments to move in the right direction. The European Movement was soon to undertake positive action. Its first aim was the creation of a European Consultative Assembly. A memorandum to this effect was delivered to the interested governments on August 18, 1948. But, although the reaction of the French and Belgian governments was positive, although they agreed to submit the proposal to the Permanent Commission of the Western European Union (the Brussels Treaty powers), one sector of resistance immediately became apparent: the British Government.

The British Government was willing to consider a European Council of Ministers whose task would be the study of certain common issues, excepting domestic economic problems and questions of defense. But it wished to have nothing to do with an assembly that would encourage agitation and spread confusion. Both Attlee and Bevin repeated the well-known arguments on the necessity of not hurrying the movement and of solving practical problems as they occurred.

> I feel [said Bevin in a parliamentary speech of September 15, 1948] that the intricacies of Western Europe are such that we had better proceed—I am not dogmatic about this—on the same principle of association of nations that we have in the Commonwealth. Britain has to be in both places; she has to be and must remain the centre of the Commonwealth itself and she must be European. It is a very difficult role to play. It is different from that of anyone else and I think that adopting the principle of an unwritten constitution, and the process of constant association step by step, by treaty and agreement, and by taking on certain things collectively instead of by ourselves, is the right way to approach this Western Union problem.

The winter of 1949 passed in study and negotiation among the Five. Finally, Bevin—who also had to consider the pressures brought to bear by a sizable number of MP's, both Conservative and Labour—gave in. And on May 5, 1949, the Statute of the Council of Europe, prepared by a committee of ambassadors, was signed; an official declaration noted:

The main feature of the Statute is the establishment of a Committee of Ministers and of a Consultative Assembly, which together will form the Council of Europe. Of these two bodies, the Committee of Ministers will provide for the development of co-operation between governments, while the Consultative Assembly will provide a means through which the aspirations of the European peoples may be formulated and expressed, the governments thus being kept continually in touch with European public opinion.*

This was not what the European federalists had hoped for. The creation of the Council of Europe was, it is true, a success for the European Movement and also, it must be remembered in passing, for Coudenhove-Kalergi; they were rewarded for their labors with this first outline for a European Parliament. But the militants in the European Movement were not satisfied. Late in February, 1949, they held their first congress in Brussels and adopted a set of principles on European policy and a plan for a European Court of the Rights of Man. A new memorandum on the Assembly was presented shortly thereafter to the ambassadors charged with working out its plans.

At the end of April, an economic conference was held at Westminster. On this occasion, the European Movement once again succeeded in getting economists and politicians as well as representatives of management and labor to participate. In good European fashion, the debates set liberals against partisans of a controlled economy, the British (concerned about maintaining their Commonwealth ties) against partisans of full European economic integration. Obviously, they would never reach total agreement. But their testimony enlarged the dossier on European economic integration and opened the way for further action aimed at free convertibility of currencies, the free circulation of goods, and also the creation of joint institutions for basic industries.

* Cited in A. H. Robertson, *The Council of Europe: Its Structure, Functions, and Achievements* 2nd ed.; (London and New York, 1961), p. 6.

Some months later, in October, 1949, the European Cultural Conference was held at Lausanne, from which emerged the College of Europe at Bruges and the European Cultural Center at Geneva.

The record of 1949 was on the whole a positive one. The European Movement had consolidated its organization and policies, it had developed and sharpened its program and had thus prepared the intellectual foundation for a new stage in European integration. These results did not, however, have much of an impact on public opinion, perhaps because of the disappointment in not attaining the breakthrough originally hoped for, but more important, because more pressing political problems dominated the scene. Europe was faced with direct threats to her security that made her inherent fragility seem still more frail and that forced her to turn to the United States.

For Soviet pressure had not lessened—quite the contrary. On the heels of the insurrectional strikes that had shaken Italy and France during the winter of 1947–48, and after the spectacular power grab in Czechoslovakia, came the Soviet attempt to take over Berlin by blockade. The operation began late in March, 1948, gradually building up to the complete closing off of the frontiers on June 10. This was hardly surprising. The adjournment *sine die* of the London Conference of Foreign Ministers at the end of 1947 had been considered a *de facto* breaking off of negotiations over Germany. So both sides thought that they were free to act as they wished. The monetary reform which the Allies instituted both in their zones of occupation and their sectors of Berlin underscored—if such emphasis was needed—the sharp division between the two Germanies. At the same time, it gave the Soviet authorities an opportunity or pretext for measures designed to liquidate the Allied enclave in the Eastern occupation zone.

Although this Berlin threat was more serious than the previous ones, because it was aimed directly at the Western Allies, this Soviet challenge did not have the desired effect. On the contrary, it gave the United States the opportunity to demonstrate not only her air power but her talent for organization, and it provoked both a stiffening of Western resistance and a regroupment of Western forces.

As a matter of fact, the interest in strengthening the new security organization set up by the Brussels Treaty had already been demonstrated before the Berlin crisis, by the establishment of a tie with the United States. The anxiety that prompted this tie stemmed particularly from the general pessimism over the debates of the Security Council. The United Nations was, in fact, paralyzed by the veto power of Security Council members. A collective-security system for defense became all the more important.

By the beginning of March, 1949, Ernest Bevin had already notified Secretary of State George Marshall that it was essential to reinforce the position of the Brussels Treaty powers; he envisioned a plan for the defense of the Atlantic together with a security system in the Mediterranean. This British move did not fail to have repercussions. The Canadian Government, which had closely followed the whole situation, publicly expressed its interest in the strengthening of Western European union. On April 29, Saint Laurent ended a report on the international situation with a discussion of the possibility of closer association among the free nations in favor of collective security, a possibility foreseen in Article 51 of the U.N. Charter:

> It may be that the free states, or some of them, will soon find it necessary to consult together on how best to establish such a collective security league. It might grow out of the plans for a Western European union now maturing.*

* *The New York Times*, April 30, 1948, p. 5.

In the United States, opinion was much the same. On the very day that the Brussels Treaty was signed—March 17, 1948—President Truman sent a message to Congress in which he declared that the Treaty deserved complete support and that he was confident the United States would give to the free nations of the world through all appropriate means the aid they needed. He said he was certain that the determination of the free nations of Europe to defend themselves would be supported by America's firm resolve to help them do so. This declaration did not imply that the United States was ready to associate with the five signatories of the Brussels Treaty or to commit herself to the obligations of a regional pact, as Bevin invited her to do. The President, as determined as he may have been, was careful. The initiative had to come from the Senate. And it came from a man whose commitment at this decisive moment symbolized the profound, almost revolutionary, development that had taken place in American public opinion, at least in the minds of her political leaders—Senator Vandenberg.

For some time, Vandenberg had been trying to find ways to get around the Soviet veto without violating the U.N. Charter. His experience in the framing of the Rio Pact helped him find the elements of a solution. The Rio Pact is set up under Articles 52, 53, and 54 of the U.N. Charter, which authorize regional agreements under certain conditions. Article 51, moreover, expressly reserves "the right of individual or collective self-defense" to each of the member states that might be the object of armed aggression, "until the Security Council has taken the measures necessary to maintain international peace and security." Vandenberg now drafted a Senate Resolution expressing the U.S. desire to limit the right of veto in the Security Council and giving the first indication of American interest in participating with Europe in a regional agreement. This resolution, developed with the help of Robert Lovett, then Under Secretary of State, was discussed with representatives of the Chiefs of Staff, the principal Congressional leaders, and the Secretary and Under Secretary of State, and was then submitted to the Senate Committee on Foreign Relations. On June 11, 1948, the Senate adopted it by 64 votes to 6.

The resolution is of great importance in the history of the Atlantic world, and it would be well for us to recall its terms. The Government of the United States, it said,

By constitutional process, should particularly pursue the following objectives within the framework of the United Nations Charter:

(1) Voluntary agreement to remove the veto from all questions involving pacific settlements of international disputes and situations, and from the admission of new members.

(2) Progressive development of regional and other collective arrangements for individual and collective self-defense in accordance with the purposes, principles, and provisions of the Charter.

(3) Association of the United States, by constitutional process, with such regional and other collective arrangements as are based on continuous and effective self-help and mutual aid, and as affect its national security.

(4) Contributing to the maintenance of peace by making clear its determination to exercise the right of individual or collective self-defense, under Article 51, should any armed attack occur affecting its national security.

(5) Maximum efforts to obtain agreements to provide the United Nations with armed forces as provided by the Charter, and to obtain agreement among member nations upon universal regulation and reduction of armaments under adequate and dependable guaranty against violation.

(6) If necessary, after adequate effort toward strengthening the United Nations, review of the Charter at an appropriate time by a General Conference called under Article 109 or by the General Assembly.*

The Senate thus declared that it was ready to consider membership of the United States in a regional collective-

* *A Decade of American Foreign Policy*, p. 1197.

security organization. It was a revolutionary declaration, although American participation in a regional pact was not without precedent. The United States was already associated in an inter-American system—to the foundation of which, in fact, she herself had greatly contributed. She had also joined in coalitions with the European nations. But she had not allowed herself to become involved in their dangerous games, and her participation had been temporary, granted merely for the duration of a war that had begun before she joined. The Vandenberg Resolution broke with this tradition of reserve in United States relations with Europe and it broke with the Monroe Doctrine—or what remained of it after two world wars—to affirm that the United States was ready to join a regional European entente. Also, it revealed that the men responsible for American policy were now aware of the obstacles to the establishment of a collective-security system that, a few years earlier, had been considered the panacea for all international ills.

The resolution voted by the Senate aimed at only a limited objective. The alliances it considered could only be military ones: It was essentially a question of setting up a regional collective-security system that would naturally mesh into a world system based on the U.N. Charter. At no point was it a question of setting up an Atlantic Community with a definitely political structure. Furthermore, the language of the resolution was subtly but deliberately cautious: American participation in any regional pact was always to be subject to the "constitutional process" of the United States, a stipulation that was understandable coming from a Senate eager to preserve its prerogatives; and the references to the U.N. Charter occurred frequently enough to make it absolutely clear that the United States had not given up hope that someday the Charter would be an effective instrument in international affairs. The only article that implied a truly new commitment on the part of the United States, Article 3, contained various carefully worded loopholes, and the Senate Foreign Relations Committee report that accompanied the resolution emphasized these loopholes even more. Clearly this "revolutionary" resolution was singularly restrained. It appears that the legislators who voted for it had not yet overcome their traditional distrust of entangling alliances, nor had they yet abandoned the hope of attaining that ultimate and ideal world order which the United States had always made the goal of its diplomacy.

Nevertheless, the mood in which the Senators passed the resolution, the conditions in which it had been formulated, and, especially, the fact that it had come from the Senate and that it had been proposed by one of the most respected leaders of the opposition party—all this helped to mark it as a new departure, and one with great symbolic value. The public paid attention only to Article 3, and Article 3 opened a new era in United States foreign policy.

Soon, Soviet pressure on Berlin forced the American Government and the Brussels Treaty powers to translate the intentions expressed in the Vandenberg resolution into a real alliance. As early as July 6, 1948, negotiations began in Washington between the Under Secretary of State, the ambassadors from the Brussels Treaty powers, and the Canadian Ambassador. The talks went on through the summer and autumn, when the foreign ministers took over, until complete agreement was reached on the principle of a defensive organization for the North Atlantic region. In December, it was decided to invite Denmark, Ireland, Norway, and Portugal to join in the alliance and to participate in the final phase of preparing a North Atlantic Treaty. Its imminent publication was announced by President Truman on January 14, 1949; two months later, on March 18, the North Atlantic Treaty was published, and, on April 4, signed in Washington.

The essential purpose of this treaty was, of course, to create a regional collective-security agreement, and its principal clauses dealt with military aspects of this security. But the

desire to justify NATO to the rest of the world, and especially
to the United Nations, led its authors not only to repeat their
adherence to the principles of the U.N. Charter but also to
express the very bases—philosophical and political—upon
which NATO was founded.

Thus, the preamble, after reaffirming the faith of the contracting parties in the goals and principles of the U.N. Charter,
spoke of the determination "to safeguard the freedom, common heritage and civilization of their peoples, founded on the
principles of democracy, individual liberty and the rule of
law," and of their desire "to promote stability and well-being
in the North Atlantic region."*

The idea of an Atlantic community was beginning to take
shape. But its outlines were still hazy in men's minds and these
references to a common good were scarcely more than rhe-
torical formulas. The nations were joining together in order
to face a common danger—it was in relation to the enemy
that they defined themselves. The strong declarations of faith
in the future of Communist society made by Soviet leaders
and their determination to reject any kind of collaboration or
exchange with the non-Communist world—which might leave
the Soviet Union open to the effects of osmosis and threaten
the Socialist experiment there as well as the world revolution
—all this forced the West European nations and the United
States to recognize that they shared democratic concepts of
social and political life.

The Soviet Government—and it was echoed by all the
Western Communist leaders—obviously gave another explanation for the North Atlantic Treaty. American imperialism—
that imperialism which, according to Lenin's dictum, is the

* A report of the Senate Committee on Foreign Relations was more ex-
plicit: "The peoples of the North Atlantic area are linked together not only
by the interdependence of their security but by a common heritage and
civilization and devotion to free institutions, based upon the principles of
democracy, individual liberty and the rule of law." (*A Decade of American
Foreign Policy*, p. 1342.)

inevitable consequence of monopolistic capitalism—bore full responsibility for a regional alliance that was a blatant instrument of aggression. But such accusations, however virulent, had no real foundation; Lester Pearson, Prime Minister of Canada, was closer to the truth when he declared, at the signing of the Treaty:

> The Atlantic Pact was born of fear and deception; of fear of the subversive and aggressive actions of communism and of the effects of these actions on our peace, our security, and our well-being; of deception in regard to the stubborn obstruction of communist states barring the way to new efforts at permitting the United Nations to function effectively as a universal security system.

The manner in which the news of the treaty was received proved further to what extent its creation had been a product of external pressure on the member states. Dean Acheson, however, still insisted, in a speech broadcast on March 18, 1949, on "the affinity and natural identity of interests of the North Atlantic powers." He affirmed that the treaty that now formally bound them together was the final outcome of 350 years of history. It rested on a common attachment to the principles "of democracy, individual liberty, and the rule of law" which flowered in the Atlantic Community, the values of which were universal. It was also the result of another unifying influence—the sea, which does not separate peoples but which unites them, through commerce, travel, and a community of interests. "For this second reason, as well as for the first," he concluded, "North America and Western Europe have formed the two halves of what is in reality one community and have maintained an abiding interest in each other."

But in addition to this historical relationship, Dean Acheson stressed at even greater length the importance of the military considerations that had led the Government of the United States to sign such a treaty, which was—and he strongly emphasized this point—a defensive arrangement. "In the compact world of today," he remarked, "the security of the United States cannot be defined in terms of boundaries and frontiers. A serious threat to international peace and security anywhere in the world is a direct concern to this country. Therefore it is our policy to help free people to maintain their integrity and independence, not only in Western Europe or in the Americas but wherever the aid we are able to provide can be effective."* This showed that the necessity for the United States to face up to the Soviet threat "everywhere" in the world—and that meant also in the Atlantic—was as important as, if not more important than, the consideration of "the affinity and identity of mutual interests."

Ernest Bevin and Robert Schuman also invoked military arguments. The treaty, Bevin declared in the House of Commons, assured Western Europe of a preponderance of power —to be used for the end of peace, security, and international order. And he emphasized as well its historical importance, which lay not so much in a political realization of an Atlantic Community as in the fact that for the first time the United States had undertaken obligations to Europe in peacetime. Robert Schuman's comments were not much different. He, too, noted the treaty's military importance; he, too, strove to show that its provisions were in no way incompatible with the United Nations Charter; and for him as well, its historical importance lay in the fact that France obtained what she had "vainly hoped for between the two wars—United States recognition that there is neither peace nor security if Europe is threatened." As for a "common heritage," he scarcely mentioned it. Rather, he remarked that if, for purposes of defense, "France joins with other democratic countries of varied polit-

* *Strengthening the Forces of Freedom: Selected Speeches and Statements of Secretary of State Acheson: February, 1949–April, 1950* (Washington: U. S. Government Printing Office, 1950), pp. 80, 82.

ical tendencies . . . she will not opt for any of those regimes—
she will remain faithful to herself."

Public opinion—as expressed in the parliaments during the
ratification debates, and in newspapers and periodicals—was
focused equally on the military and political aspects of the
treaty—the primary question being whether it really was a
contribution to peace or whether it did not actually aggravate
the Cold War by cementing the division of the world into two
blocs. This argument, constantly harped on by the Communists, was taken up in Europe by individuals and groups
on the left that in postwar years had often shown their distrust
of the United States. Their criticisms, which had been heard
before at the time of debates on the Marshall Plan, were symp-
tomatic of a widespread European attitude.

The Western Europe of 1945 was socialist, despite the fact
that no one could say what kind of socialism it was. The
young believed in it, as might be expected, but mature men
returning from imprisonment or deportation also did—the
men who had fought in the Resistance, or at the front, or on
the homefront, under bullets, shells, and bombs—everyone
who, viewing the ruins about him, measured the extent of the
disaster and became aware of the solidarity created by common misery and sufferings. They were "on the left," by
which they understood that their ideal was a social democracy,
a socialism that would eliminate economic feudalism and guarantee each person not only political liberty, but also economic
freedom—that is, material security. Marxist formulas were no
doubt used, but they were usually stylistic mannerisms, the
effect of more or less well digested readings or of habits acquired almost unconsciously—like the man who spoke prose
without knowing it. Orthodox Marxism, although revised and
completed by Lenin and the Soviet thinkers, belonged to the
Communists. West European socialism, with its national
nuances varying from country to country, was closer to the
humanitarian socialism of the nineteenth century, albeit modi-

fied by the influences of Proudhon, of Fabianism, and even of
Marx as seen through Bernstein, Jaurès, Kautsky, Guesde, or
Léon Blum.

Now this self-styled "Europe of the left" had great trouble
understanding America, the more so as it was subject to that
instinctive distrust the poor have of the rich, and the weak of
the powerful. The instability that marked the political life of
the Fourth Republic, the tension persisting in Italy, where the
Christian Democrats had to deal with a highly organized
Communist Party, England's continuing economic difficulties
—these European elements hardly encouraged a favorable
view of the transatlantic ally who appeared to enjoy, in all
complacence, the contemplation of his material success.

Besides, what was known about the United States? A few
fragmentary impressions gained through books by European
travelers in America, books which too often reflected the
prejudices of the traveler, which—instead of explaining the
everyday America of the man who has to work hard to make
a living, or a searching, thoughtful, creative America—described an America of huge modern cities, slums, and gang-
ster movies, of Harlem and the Negro problem, of nightclubs
and funeral homes, of the Kinsey Report. It was an image
drawn from chance readings, and also from chance encounters
with Americans on the Continent. The contact with American
soldiers during and after the war had not always been pleasant.
Both in England and on the Continent, people commented on
the complete lack of discipline and the drunkenness of the
Americans. And then came the tourists, not all of whom were
ready or willing to appreciate, as the cultivated European
would have wished it, the marvels of the old world. Organized
tours with those never-changing itineraries made the European
smile; he could not understand what it was that compelled
the American visitor to see as much as possible in so short a
time. And American college students, both good and bad, who

came to study and did not always take their work seriously, were considered "typical."

Other impressions were added to those gained in these personal contacts. Certain types of publicity violated cherished European habits and susceptibilities. People who dealt with the American administration were disgusted by its slowness and red tape; the precautions taken before issuing even the simplest tourist visa were irritating; business and trade practices differed radically from those of Europe and intensified existing distrust. And finally, there was the America as revealed in films, magazines, and newspapers. In Hollywood productions and the smug self-satisfaction of many American magazines, the European found grist for his mill, confirmation of his prejudices against an image of America that had been established before the war—a capitalist, materialist America, disturbing in her innocent strength, embarrassing in her generosity, and tiresome in her naïveté.

More enlightened observers, of course, insisted that these impressions of the United States were not accurate, that, for example, American capitalism after the Wall Street crash and the New Deal only slightly resembled the picture Europeans had of it. But their testimony and their warnings had little effect, for they ran counter to the general current of public opinion, which was the stronger since the reactions of the man in the street and those of the intellectual seemed to converge. Tocqueville, whose perspicacity American intellectuals admire, had given this advice: "One must take care not to judge newborn societies according to the ideas drawn from societies that no longer exist. That would be unjust, because these societies, so prodigiously different one from the other, are not comparable." But it was not Tocqueville but rather Duhamel who was read in France in 1949—who reminded America, the land of efficiency, that all the "basic ideas" came from Europe; and Mauriac—who disdainfully called America a "technocracy"; or Sartre—who tersely affirmed that "an American is

never taken with a European idea." And it was not to the
subtle and clever Denis Brogan that the British public looked
for an explanation of the United States or of American foreign policy, but to the mass-circulation newspapers, still harp-
ing on the old themes that had their roots in the long years of
Anglo-American rivalry. Very few Europeans had read the
great American historian Carlton Hayes:

> The American frontier is a frontier of European or "Western"
> culture. This culture, however modified by or adapted to pe-
> culiar geographical and social conditions in America or else-
> where, is still, in essential respects, the culture and hence a
> continuous bond of the regional community of nations on both
> sides of the Atlantic.*

Europeans, then, were hostile to the North Atlantic Pact
and lacked confidence in the United States, but this did not
mean that they were ready to support the Soviet Union. The
main point was that they did not wish to make a choice between the two. Communism did not labor under the burden
of condemnation, as did Hitlerism. It might, after this period
of revolution and conquest, remember its first role, that of a
liberating force; the Soviet Union could evolve; there was still
hope. The truth was that the most resolute enemies of the
U.S.S.R., and those most determined to resist Soviet advances,
were found nearest the line of demarcation. As one moved
further away from the threatened frontier and closer to the
Atlantic coast, fear lessened, judgments became blurred, and
hope was renewed. Paradoxically, it was in the eastern part of
the Continent that the Atlantic Pact would find its warmest
adherents and in the western part its most stringent critics.

In addition to those who were deliberately hostile, there
were others who had reservations about the efficacy of a treaty
that depended on how its signatories would interpret its

* "The American Frontier—Frontier of What?" in *American Historical
Review*, Vol. LI (January, 1946).

clauses. Could Europe be sure that the Americans would honor their obligations and immediately come to the aid of the victims of aggression? The skeptics observed pointedly that there were certain difficulties. The implementation of the treaty clauses was subject to American constitutional restrictions, which meant that the Senate reserved the authority to decide on what action to take in each particular case. It did not intend to permit automatic implementation of the treaty, which it considered tantamount to turning the United States over to its European allies. This legislative authority, which was very clearly spelled out by government officials and emphasized in the press, was naturally the subject of much discussion in Europe. An article by "Sirius" in *Le Monde* summed it up on the eve of the signing of the Pact:

Certain Europeans who are familiar with the nature of American institutions and customs are concerned with preventing a possible, if not probable, misunderstanding. They are perfectly willing for the Americans to raise questions about the strength and dependability of their allies. But, in their turn, they would like to know when and how Europe will be protected. Is the impenetrable atomic curtain anything more than a myth? Even supposing that it is a reality, will the United States use this frightening device early enough to paralyze aggression? The projected agreement does not say. Even if it did, the guarantee would be far from absolute; there is not, there has probably never been, an automatic entry into war on the part of a democratic nation and of a people devoted to peace. Is it necessary to recall here that a precisely worded treaty joined France to Czechoslovakia? And since it is understood that an attack against any one of the signatories of the Atlantic Pact is an attack against them all, what would happen if the United States alone were attacked on her Pacific coast and appealed to the automatic clauses of the treaty? Would we see European armies set off immediately to the East? Let us at least be honest enough to ask the question.*

* "Le Pacte Atlantique et la paix," *Le Monde*, March 17, 1949.

Sirius was not the only one in France to voice this warning. Etienne Gilson, in the columns of *Le Monde*, said much the same thing, quoting some remarks made by James Reston in *The New York Times* to prove his point. According to Gilson, Reston had said this:

> The treaty contains both a solemn principle and a way of getting around it. It is conceived to protect the Atlantic Community against armed attack. It obliges the signatories to take up arms "immediately" against an armed attack threatening the security of the region, but at the same time it leaves each country free to decide for itself: (a) if an "armed attack" has taken place—for example, if a Communist rebellion in Greece is an armed attack; (b) what action to take against this attack (a diplomatic protest is an "action"); (c) if the armed attack really threatens the "security" of the North Atlantic zone.

Gilson concluded, after having recalled Wilson's failures: "It is henceforth inexcusable for any Frenchman not to know that a treaty with the United States does not oblige our friends to go one inch beyond the precise interpretation they may choose to give its provisions."*

The debate is interesting because it is representative of the attitude of a section of European and American opinion, and, still more, because it reveals reservations about the treaty on both sides of the Atlantic: Obligations were undertaken because it did not appear possible to do otherwise, but the hope that one would never be compelled to make so grave a decision—or that one would retain one's freedom of decision—was the factor that persuaded the American public to accept the treaty and finally swayed the Senate.

On the European side, many people, including the most devoted partisans of the treaty, had mixed feelings, divided between concern over these reservations in the United States (after all, her protection was needed) and the uneasiness this

* *Le Monde*, March 26, 1949.

extremely dynamic and powerful ally inspired. Europe wanted to keep her independence. Europe thought of herself—and was encouraged to do so by the movement for European integration—as being capable of creating a third force between East and West. She did not wish to be beholden to the United States—she herself was the fount and creative source of an ancient and unique civilization. It was not surprising that references to the "common heritage" were rare, although here and there there were a few: "They have formed the club because they are old associates," wrote *The Economist*. "They are not associates because they have formed the club."* Generally, much more attention was paid to what divided the treaty members than to what they had in common. The basic attitude was one of resignation to the necessary and inevitable.

Who was to be included in this club? Where were the frontiers of the Alliance? Would Italy be a member? On the very day the treaty was published, the Italian Chamber of Deputies, after extremely violent debates, approved the principle of Italian participation in the Atlantic Alliance. But the English, in particular, had some doubts on the matter. If the Italian peninsula were included in the Atlantic Pact, should Greece and Turkey, the two countries on whose behalf the United States had become involved in European affairs to begin with, be left out? As for the eventual participation of West Germany, all the members were in agreement: It was out of the question. Did it follow, then, that one frontier of the Atlantic world was on the Rhine?

There was also much discussion on the limits of the application of the treaty. From the point of view of the Charter, the obligations of the United States were general and nonregional, Hamilton Fish Armstrong noted in an article in *Foreign Affairs* in the fall of 1948. And is it not difficult to

* "Atlantic Pact," *The Economist*, March 19, 1949, pp. 498-99.

define satisfactorily the limits of a region when the political situation is so fluid? In April, 1949, Armstrong, who was not alone in his views, raised the issue again. What would be the duties of great nations that found themselves associated in several regional groupings? To what extent would they share responsibility for the colonial policies of their allies? What attitude should be adopted when troubles arose involving another alliance system? Moreover, how could one keep those on the outside of the treaty from feeling that they had been pushed to one side and being tempted to pass over to the other side?

There is only one conclusion to be drawn from an analysis of the climate of opinion that prevailed on the eve of the North Atlantic Treaty. No real will to create an Atlantic Community existed at the moment that governments and parliaments were rallying to the Atlantic Pact. The twelve associated states seemed to be more jealous of their independence than happy over the prospects of collaboration now opening up in the Atlantic world, and some of them felt a part of that world because of political circumstances rather than because of a geographical imperative.

There was no thought at this time of opposing an "Atlantic Community" to a "European Union." American statesmen were careful to show that they had no other objective than to bring to Europe the security necessary for her economic recovery. The Atlantic Pact made possible the fulfillment of the European Recovery Program, whose objective remained the economic and political integration of Western Europe. As for the directors of the European Movement—some of whom, in particular the Federalists, had never missed a chance to say that a united Europe should be integrated into still larger systems—they saw in the Atlantic Pact simply the strengthening of Europe's capacity to resist. They knew, moreover, that the campaigns directed against the Atlantic Pact were aimed equally at the programs under way for Europe's political consolidation and consequently were careful not to do anything that might encourage divisive maneuvers. The United States gave Europe the military protection necessary for the realization of the plan that totally absorbed them. They asked nothing more.

Only Canada, torn between the historic ties that bound it to Great Britain and the geographical attraction of the American continent, seemed to see in the future of the Atlantic Community a means of surmounting her national contradictions and of dissolving it in a vast grouping that would include all those countries identified with Western civilization. "Our Atlantic Union," Lester Pearson wrote, "must give rise to a desire for, and habits of, cooperation that go beyond the immediate crisis. It is by aiming at an amelioration of the living conditions of our peoples that we can create the basis for a true collaboration, which will render formal agreements unnecessary."

But the other allies did not look so far ahead. Europe, which was benefiting from U.S. economic aid, simply needed the military protection America was ready to give because it was in her interest to do so. For the rest, each country was involved with her own worries—and they were not negligible.

The Democratic Administration, although strengthened in the Presidential elections of 1948, was faced with an increasingly vigorous Republican opposition, which exploited, at one and the same time, the weaknesses of a party long in power and the feeling of insecurity to which the Hiss affair, the end of America's atomic monopoly, and Mao Tse-tung's victory over America's ally Chiang Kai-shek had given rise. France, where the break-up of the tripartite system and the resurgence of the old political parties had led to a frittering away of strength (all the more dangerous as the Communist Party, excluded from all participation in government, still represented about one-quarter of the electorate), was becoming enmeshed in a colonial war in Indochina that by its very nature was quite unpopular, and during which one government after another, all without effective power or a political majority, was defeated. In Great Britain, the Labour Party, having come to the end of its earlier reform program, lost its momentum and popularity, for that part of the middle class that, unlike the workers, had not really benefited from social reforms, was less and less inclined to suffer the restrictions of an austerity program. And Britain too had increasing difficulties beyond its island frontiers: in the Middle East, where relations with Egypt were entering a new crisis period; in Africa, where the race-relations problem became more acute every day. Italy continued to survive, in one way or another, preserving that uncertain equilibrium into which she had settled right after the war, burdened by the seemingly permanent contradiction between her economic potential and the number of mouths to feed.

Now, the strength of an alliance is a function of the strength of the nations associated in it, and its unity depends on the credit and authority of each government in its own country. As the governments in each case were more or less unstable, and, moreover, as some of the most delicate national problems, both economic and political, could not be solved either within the framework of national competence or within national frontiers, the North Atlantic Treaty was to suffer, on the one hand, from the resistance within each country to the application of decisions taken in the interest of the whole alliance, and, on the other hand, from the interpenetration of national interests, the transfer of unresolved national problems to the international stage, which burdened it with problems it was not yet prepared to deal with and on which there was no international agreement, even in principle.

In fact, nothing cemented this newly created alliance but the Soviet Union.

{ 4 }

Stormy Dialogues Across the Atlantic

One of the principal motives behind the initiative taken by member states of the Brussels Treaty had been the desire to obtain from the United States the military and financial support necessary for the organization of Europe's defense. It is therefore not surprising that no sooner was the North Atlantic Treaty signed than the member states made overtures to Washington for such aid.

The American Administration was favorably disposed to these requests, but it also had to take account of the objections that had been raised in the United States during the debate over the ratification of the pact: Its opponents had tried to force the Administration into declaring that the treaty implied no pledge of arms for the allies. The Administration had replied that it did not contain this obligation, thereby cutting off what might have been a most dangerous debate—and for good reason. But as soon as the treaty was ratified, the President asked Congress to approve a $1.4 billion program of military aid; he obtained most of this, not without difficulty, in September.

With this battle won, it was possible to proceed with the

establishment of NATO institutions and with the working
out of a common concept for North Atlantic defense and for
basic strategic plans. The autumn and winter of 1949–50 were
devoted to this task. But very early, the planners came up
against various problems that forced them to modify their
initial projects and to widen the NATO infrastructure. At
the first session of the Organization, it had been planned to
establish—along with a Council made up of defense ministers
of the member states—a Military Committee and five regional
strategic groups. Several months later, a Committee of Economic and Financial Defense, made up of the ministers of
finance, and a Military Production Committee were added.
Then, in the spring of 1950, after a plan for the integrated
defense of the Atlantic zone had been adopted, the member
states were forced to evaluate more completely the financial
implications and organizational problems of this integrated
defense; a permanent council of assistant foreign ministers
was organized and given responsibility for coordinating work
in the military, economic, and financial spheres—the objective
always being a progressive and balanced growth of the
NATO forces. Once created, this permanent council developed according to its own logic and inevitably caught up
the NATO states in a mesh of integration. For it is impossible
to organize a common defense without partial integration of
national armies, and this, since it involves measures of rationalization in all sectors (particularly in production), directly
affects the national economies, making all sorts of budgetary
readjustments necessary.

While the governments and general staffs forged ahead
with this organization of the Western world's defense, tension was mounting in some of the allied countries. A "peace
offensive" was developing in Europe, started by the "peace
partisans" and inspired and directed by the Communists. The
Stockholm Appeal, demanding a prohibition of all atomic
weapons and condemning as criminal any government that

would dare to use them first, found numerous supporters, all the more so since President Truman had announced at the beginning of the year his decision to go ahead with the manufacture of thermonuclear weapons. Europe, ever more convinced of its weakness and of the permanent superiority of the U.S.S.R. over the United States in conventional weapons, feared that the latter would be led to balance this disequilibrium by recourse to atomic weapons. She feared, then, that in the event of war, her liberation would be achieved only at the price of total destruction, and she reacted against this prospect with some vigor. It was in this climate that the "neutralist" movement was to develop. It had already been seen in certain observations made in France at the time of the North Atlantic Treaty. Had not Etienne Gilson spoken of the "armed neutrality" of Europe? A year earlier, Claude Bourdet had campaigned in favor of a similar policy. In 1950, the movement grew in scope: The *ohne mich* slogan had considerable success in Germany; Nenni and the left-wing Socialists were also in favor of a neutralist policy. But it was in France especially that neutralism was gaining strength. *Le Monde* undertook a real campaign in its behalf and drew support from the groups focusing around the magazines *Esprit* and *France Observateur*.

To what extent did this neutralism differ from classic neutrality? It is difficult to say, and it is not certain that the "neutralists" knew, since they used the terms interchangeably. But certainly it did not appear that they had considered all the consequences of their policy, nor that they had estimated the military burden it implied. At any rate, theories about neutralism differed from one person to the next, although all had the same objective in mind: the disruption of the Atlantic Pact, which was seen as a road to war. Claude Bourdet expressed the basic thesis well: The security of a country or of a group of countries depends in the final analysis on three elements: material strength, moral unity, and the danger that that country or group of countries poses for other nations.

The latter might be called the "provocation factor." This security would, then, be defined "as a mathematical quotient: It is the product of material power multiplied by moral unity, the total divided by the provocation factor." According to Bourdet, neutrality would reduce Europe's provocation factor: "It would offer the Russian General Staff the option to weigh the advantages and disadvantages of invading Europe, while on the other hand Russia would be militarily obligated to invade an Atlantic Europe immediately. Moreover, European neutrality would enormously increase the moral unity of the nation."*

The purpose of this neutralism, thus, was not only to disengage France and Europe from power politics, but also to leave a choice open between Communism and American capitalist civilization. The argument held a certain attraction, but its political influence was limited. First of all, its disciples soon came up against opposition from the Communist movement, which insisted on a clear choice between socialism and capitalism and for whom there was no third way. But, also, a conversion of France and Europe to neutralism implied a renunciation of world responsibilities, and that was to demand a true *volte face*.

While all this went on, the Korean War broke out. The shock of the invasion in Korea was a great one, for all of Europe. What people had considered improbable, because it was convenient to do so, had come to pass—i.e., an overt act of aggression—and it was immediately imagined it could happen elsewhere. It was natural to compare Korea and a divided Germany. But no preparation had been made for facing a possible Soviet aggression. The fourteen allied divisions in Europe and Germany, a certain number of them seriously understaffed, were neither integrated under a single command nor deployed with a view to an operative engagement. Their lines

* Claude Bourdet, in *L'Observateur*, June 8, 1950, p. 23.

of communication, which ran parallel to the front, could be rapidly cut, and their airports, unprotected by ground forces, could be rapidly occupied.

The anxiety aroused by the atomic-weapons race and focused primarily against the United States was now succeeded by a fear of Soviet occupation. For several weeks, the Korean War re-established unity in the Atlantic camp around the United States, which alone had the means to stand up to the U.S.S.R. Europeans were grateful to her for taking up the challenge and for demonstrating her attachment to the principle of collective security; they were reassured by her vigorous measures to mobilize her army, which she had dangerously reduced. In September, the NATO Council unanimously adopted a "forward-looking strategy" for Europe—agreeing to meet any aggression in the East so as to protect the greatest possible area of Europe and to set up a unified force under a single command for this purpose.

This new strategy did not only mean an acceleration of NATO's work, but also an increased effort on the part of each ally. It also reopened the problem of German rearmament. How would it be possible to plan an advanced defense system, including in it a large part of German territory, without involving the Germans themselves? One could not imagine leaving them free of obligations, protected by French, British, Belgian, or Dutch troops who would get themselves killed in their defense. If an augmentation of military effort was required, each of the beneficiaries had to play his part. This became the argument of the United States when she proposed to associate Germany in the defense of Europe. The proposition—which was, after all, the logical conclusion of any objective analysis of the situation—was a challenge for Europe, at once disturbing and stimulating.

Germany was, indeed, no longer considered an enemy country. The awareness of the impossibility of agreeing with

the Soviet Union on the economic and political reconstruction of Central Europe had led to a step-by-step reversal of
alliances. Running the risk of losing all of Germany, the allies
had decided to permit that part of Germany they controlled
to take its destiny into its own hands once again while binding it as solidly as possible to Western Europe. Shortly after
the creation of the combined Anglo-American zone, the allies
brought Western Germany into the Organization for European Economic Cooperation. The crises of the monetary reform and the Berlin Blockade led them to recognize, within
the framework of a formally defined occupation agreement,
the existence of a West German state. The "Basic Law,"
which a Parliamentary Council had worked on for many
months, went into effect on May 23, 1949. In the fall, after
elections had brought the Christian Democrats to power,
Theodor Heuss was elected President of the new Federal
Republic of Germany, and Konrad Adenauer became its
Chancellor.

The juridical situation of the new republic was, it is true,
ambiguous. The governments of France, the United Kingdom, and the United States had kept supreme authority for
themselves, with particular power in the following areas: "disarmament and demilitarization; controls in regard to the Ruhr,
restitution, reparations, decartelization, deconcentration, non-
discrimination in trade matters, foreign interests in Germany,
and claims against Germany; foreign affairs, including international agreements made by or in behalf of Germany; and
control over foreign trade and exchange." The sovereignty of
the Federal Republic was thus expressly limited. It was a temporary solution imposed by circumstances—that is, by the
division of Germany. The Basic Law declared in its preamble
that the "German people" of the *Laender* included within the
frontiers of the Federal Republic were acting "on behalf of
those Germans to whom participation was denied." And
again, Article 146 announced that the Basic Law "shall cease

to be in force on the day on which a constitution adopted by a free decision of the German people comes into force."

Behind the ambiguity, the hope of going beyond this temporary solution was clear, a hope expressed in a passage of the preamble that speaks of the desire of the German people "to contribute to world peace as a full and equal member of a united Europe." It was through the creation of this "united Europe" that the German people hoped to recover both rights equal to those of the other European peoples and the strong influence necessary for reunification. The policy of Chancellor Adenauer and the Christian Democratic Union was clearly established: They would be "Europeans." Their choice, however, was not approved unanimously. Adenauer had to reckon with the resistance of the small "Liberal" Party and especially of the Social Democrats, who, influenced by Kurt Schumacher, saw this Western orientation as an abandonment of the possibility of reunification, which they considered the precondition for the political rehabilitation of Germany. The simultaneous creation of the German Democratic Republic heavily underscored the division of the country and gave comfort to the Chancellor's critics. Any concession to the Western allies would be considered as an error, if not a crime, insofar as it rendered more difficult the negotiations they still believed possible with the Soviet Union on the settlement of the German question.

The position of the Federal Republic vis-à-vis the allies was less weak than might at first have appeared, for they could not ignore the pressures to which Chancellor Adenauer was subject in his own country nor the burdens weighing on his European policy. They were thus led, by the constant fear of a new Rapallo, to grant Germany more and more of the equality she was seeking and to reduce the restrictions imposed by the occupation. It was in this spirit that they invited the Federal Republic to join the Council of Europe. "A United Europe cannot live without the help and strength of

Germany," said Winston Churchill in August, 1949. "One of the most practical reasons for pressing forward with the creation of a European assembly was that it provided an effective means, and possibly the only immediately effective means, of associating a democratic and free Germany with the Western democracies."* It would have been impossible to put it more clearly.

The invitation to the Federal Republic, held up by the debate over the simultaneous admission of the Saar (demanded by the French), was finally issued at the end of March, 1950. Admitted as an associate member, Germany was not long in obtaining the status of a full member in 1951.

But before this, a spectacular gesture had been made by France to tie France and Germany more strongly together and to give the European idea a basis in reality. On May 9, 1950, Robert Schuman declared that the French Government proposed to place all French and German production of coal and steel under the jurisdiction of a single common authority, in an organization that would also be open to other European countries:

> The pooling of coal and steel production will immediately assure the establishment of a common base for economic development, the first stage of European Federation, and will change the destiny of those regions that have so long been dedicated to the manufacture of weapons of war, of which they have been the most constant victims.†

The idea was not new. The "Europeans" had from the beginning been concerned with the creation of a common market. The motion on political economy adopted by the European Union of Federalists at its Montreux Congress in 1947 had affirmed that there was no other effective solution

---

* Council of Europe, Consultative Assembly. Reports of the First Session (1949), 6th Sitting, August 17.

† Cited in C. A. Colliard, *Droit international et Histoire diplomatique*, I, 761–62.

to the social and economic problems of Europe than "the institution of an economic federation, implying the abandonment to a federal authority of part of the economic powers now held by sovereign states."* The motion had also stated that it was important to realize a "system of structural planning," as well as a decentralization of economic power and a division of labor. The resolution adopted at the Hague Congress of Europe had also mentioned the need for a common program in key industries. And, at the Westminster Conference of 1949, the basic industries commission, presided over by André Philip, had asked for the creation of common institutions in four sectors: coal, iron and steel, electricity, and transportation. (By "common institutions" was meant a public European institution that would have as its aim the formulation of general policy for the four industries; a "consultative body," including representatives of management, labor, and the "public interest"; and "industrial ententes," to bring business leaders into contact with one another.) The Council of Europe had also taken up this problem during its debates in the summer and autumn of 1949. Bonnefous and Philip had both insisted that key industries like coal and steel be placed under international administration. At the end of the same year, the economic commission of the Consultative Assembly had disregarded all reservations expressed over this project and voted for the creation of international "European companies" under the control of an "Office of European Companies," itself an agency of the Council of Europe.

The debates in the Council of Europe had been the expression of two different preoccupations, whose conclusions to a certain extent coincided. First, the rebuilding of the European economy, in particular of the iron and steel industry, was contributing to a general fear of a rebirth of economic feudalism. A new agreement between forge-masters was not

* *Rapport du Premier Congrès*, p. 129.

wanted, for it was thought that it would lead to reduced production in order to maintain price levels, when, on the contrary, it was necessary to stimulate consumption. The obvious solution was to place the steel and coal industries under the control of a public authority. Secondly, the plans of European federalists were meeting with resistance; they realized that their efforts to create a European political authority and to strengthen the powers of the Consultative Assembly vis-à-vis the Committee of Ministers were being opposed not only in the committee itself, but also by a majority of the Assembly. This opposition led them to fall back on functional solutions. Perhaps it would be possible, by consenting to a sector-by-sector integration, to persuade the nations to agree to a progressive limitation on their sovereignty for the benefit of supranational organs, and thus to construct by stages that European federation which was the final objective of their efforts.

These various plans also had the virtue of offering a means of surmounting the traditional Franco-German antagonism. A Germany that openly linked its future to a united Europe posed a delicate problem for the French Government: If one wished to accept Germany as an associate in the new Europe, one could no longer maintain the victor-vanquished relationship. How, for example, was one to assure some measure of control over the Ruhr while refusing to discuss the status of the Saar? On the other hand, was the new Europe an instrument to be used exclusively to give form and meaning to the aspirations of a reconstructed Germany? Why not create, the Federal Republic had asked, in a memorandum on the Saar of March, 1950, an "international authority"? Would it not be possible, in order to take into account the economic interpenetration of the Saar, Lorraine, and southern Germany, to consider a special customs union? Chancellor Adenauer also alluded, more than once, to a Franco-German union that would put an end to obsolete national rivalries. Schuman could not remain insensitive to his suggestions, particularly since the theme of a Saar-Lorraine-Ruhr association had been broached in the past. But how did one put these ideas into practice?

It was at this point that Jean Monnet entered the scene once again. The influence exercised by the general commissioner for France's economic "Plan" by far exceeded the limits of his official position. His work on the modernization plan—which he had modestly defined as "a method of working in common, an inventory of resources and needs in productive equipment, a program of action with orders of priority"—had given him a broad view of the potentials and needs of the French economy, and had enabled him to offer a working program to those responsible for the conduct of national affairs. Thus he was in constant contact with the most diverse groups in business and in politics, and in the course of his international career he had created a network of relations that the inevitable interpenetration of the Monnet and Marshall plans had helped to tighten still further. But Monnet, unlike many others—and this is one of his most characteristic traits—had not allowed his activities to dominate him, nor did he become imprisoned in the web of his connections. In a position where he could both act and observe, he had learned to take that long view of events which makes it possible to understand their essence. And around him there had gathered a remarkable group of invaluable assistants.

In this spring of 1950, Jean Monnet felt—as did others, but he perhaps even more clearly—the need for France to take a bold initiative.* The internal divisions of Europe was a factor in the tension between the Soviet Union and the United States; its unification would contribute to the maintenance of the

* For a recapitulation of the origins of the Schuman Plan, I have relied on Pierre Gerbet's excellent article "Genèse du Plan Schuman," *Revue française de science politique*, July–September, 1956. See also Jacques Freymond, *The Saar Conflict* (New York: Frederick A. Praeger, 1960).

peace. But progress toward unity was being prevented by national oppositions. In the Council of Europe, the Consultative Assembly, kept on the fringes of activity by the Committee of Ministers, could scarcely do more than state its wishes and show its impatience. Attempts to accelerate European integration in the OEEC had not proved satisfactory either. The OEEC responded to Paul Hoffman's appeal, made in the fall of 1949, for the creation of a great common European market by means of a customs union, with vague preparatory measures to reduce quantitative restrictions and to lift trade barriers. Faced with the failure of these international organizations, it was up to a single country, a single government, to give the impulse that might stir the imagination and crystallize public opinion.

Monnet's intervention at this point was a brilliant tactical maneuver. Not only did he choose the crucial sector of industry in which to make the integration effort, and not only did he define the modalities of this integration and outline the institutions to be created, but original as his formula for the Coal and Steel Authority may have been, the tactics Monnet employed were even more striking. Up to the last minute, secrecy was rigorously observed; all the preparations were made by a small team working under the strictest controls; there were no negotiations with interested political or economic groups; nothing was communicated to the allied governments that might give them the impression that a decisive gesture was being prepared. Then, as soon as the plan was presented to the cabinet (which put its complete confidence in the Minister of Foreign Affairs), the public was informed. The effect was immediate and profound. France had recaptured the diplomatic initiative. It was she who would lead Europe to unity.

The climate of opinion created by the launching of the Schuman Plan seemed favorable to advancing the policy of German rearmament. The United States wished to exploit the situation immediately, the more so as she was convinced (even before the Korean War) of the need for Europe and her Atlantic allies to ensure the military cooperation of Germany. But the game was harder than originally imagined. All the arguments mustered in favor of German rearmament, logical as they were, met with extremely strong resistance. World War II was too close, the memory of the destruction and of the occupation still too vivid. If the British Government, after an initial reserve, was disposed to accept the United States point of view, the French ministers made it clear that they considered it impossible to obtain a popular French majority in favor of German rearmament—a move that together with the entry of the Federal Republic into NATO would complete the reversal of alliances. French public opinion was not yet ready to make the leap.

These French objections, occurring at a moment of crisis when everyone feared that the struggle in Korea might degenerate into a general conflict, would have carried more weight if the French Government had been in a position to guarantee an appreciable increase in its own contribution to European defense. But France was involved in Indochina and could not put her forces at NATO's disposal. Under these conditions—and because it was necessary to end the impasse that had come only a few months after the encouraging beginnings of the Schuman Plan—René Pleven, adopting the pragmatism of his colleague in the Foreign Affairs Ministry, advanced a proposal for an entirely European army in which Germany would participate. While Germany would have every chance to be on an equal footing with France in a NATO dominated by the United States, the European formula allowed for some French control over Germany's reintegration into the Western defense system. It was hoped thus to attenuate the risks of German rearmament. This European army would also make it possible—or so it was hoped—to persuade the French public to accept a revolutionary reversal in national policy. Pleven's formula seemed, therefore, to contain everything needed to secure U.S. approval and to calm the fears of his own countrymen.

But the possibility of German rearmament caused concern not only among the officials of national governments. Throughout Europe, in France in particular—as well as in Germany, for that matter—the issue provoked a new burst of feverish excitement, which the Soviet Union and the Communist parties did not fail to encourage and exploit. The autumn and winter of 1950–51 were particularly difficult. The entire world, but especially the United States and her allies, were watching the developments in Korea with acute anxiety. A brilliant American military campaign had been followed, after the crossing of the 38th Parallel, by a sudden offensive of Chinese "volunteers," who at first seemed invincible. These events gave rise to contradictory reactions in Europe and the United States. As the war progressed, anxiety and anger seemed to infect Europe. It was feared the United States might commit too many troops to a minor conflict, to the detriment of the more important protection of Europe. Certain moves, such as the crossing of the 38th Parallel, were criticized although the United Nations had approved them. It was thought that these actions had provoked China and led to a widening of the conflict and increased the risks of a general war.

In addition, the fear of German rearmament led to a new interpretation of Soviet policy in some quarters. After all, it was argued, the Soviet Union had not intervened in Korea. She had been content to support North Korea's position in the United Nations and to provide it with matériel. She had not become openly involved in either Asia or in Europe, where she nonetheless had military superiority. The reason for this, it was said, was that Stalin was not ready to risk open war, that he was more "reasonable" than his critics claimed. If the West decided to rearm Germany, he would feel provoked. This was not a new argument. It had already been advanced at the time of the North Atlantic Treaty. Nevertheless it carried weight.

All in all, Europe—or at least the non-Communist European public—was at one and the same time attracted to and intimidated by American dynamism. She wished it were possible to capture that energy and direct it as she wished; she called on the United States for help and repulsed her simultaneously; American activities were encouraged, but their consequences were feared. During the fall and winter, the European members of NATO strove to convince the United States that only the sending of American troops to Europe would convince them of the United States' determination to commit herself fully if necessary. It was up to the Americans to fill the void created by the absence of German troops. Yet simultaneously, Europe asked these same Americans fighting in Korea to hold back there in order to obviate a further involvement. The British Government in particular, trying (through the intermediary of the Indian Government) to maintain contact with the People's Republic of China, preached moderation to Washington. It was only with great difficulty that the American Government persuaded its allies to vote for the resolution condemning China as an aggressor.

This attitude on the part of the European allies, all the more painful since American civilization itself often was the real target of the attack on government policy, was not appreciated in the United States. Americans did not want to hear talk of concessions to a country that had deliberately begun the hostilities. What they did want was that the allies make a greater effort to share in a common defense. "The slowness of European rearmament, and in particular France's hesitations," wrote *The New York Times*, shortly after the November elections in which the Republicans recaptured some lost ground, "seem to have given rise to the feeling that the

United States is bearing too heavy a burden of obligations."* Ex-President Hoover was even more direct:

> Competent observers are daily raising the serious question as to whether these nations, outside of Great Britain, have the will to fight, or even the will to preparedness. The actions and statements of their own leaders give little evidence of any real determination. . . . The time has come when the American people should speak out in much stronger tones than the diplomatic phrases of conference halls.†

In a second speech at the beginning of December, 1950, he spoke still more clearly:

> It is clear that the United Nations are defeated in Korea. It is also clear that other non-Communist nations did not or could not respond to the United Nations call for arms to Korea. It is clear that the United Nations cannot mobilize substantial military forces. It is clear that Continental Europe has not in the three years of our aid developed that unity of purpose, and that will power necessary for its own defense. It is clear that our British friends are flirting with appeasement of Communist China. It is clear that the United Nations is in a fog of debate and indecision on whether to appease or not to appease.

Herbert Hoover thus expressed what a great number of Americans felt, the sense of being exploited and hoodwinked by ingrates who allowed themselves the luxury of lecturing to America. All the talk of Atlantic solidarity and a common civilization was nothing more than a trap. Of what use had the Marshall dollars been? To finance costly and inefficient economic and social experiments. Why was there such a noticeable difference between American and British productivity rates? Not only was British equipment outmoded, but the ancient work methods and habits the Labour Government

---

* Editorial, November 12, 1950.
† *Documents on International Affairs: 1949–50* (London: Oxford University Press, 1953), pp. 82-83.

had been unable to modify were obsolete as well. And would social tensions have persisted in France if French employers had transcended the limits of "bourgeois" and "capitalist" concepts of human relations that Americans had long since abandoned? As for European intellectuals, who were always butting in to give lessons, their concept of American life was a caricature; they were not aware of the changes of American cultural life and the work done in the great universities. America was proud of its great scientists in all branches of learning who, whether native born or not, could be considered American patriots.

This explosion of American anger was a reply to the criticism that had been coming out of Europe since the war, and especially since the launching of the Marshall Plan. For months, there had been a feeling that everything was about to blow up. The double crisis provoked by the Korean War and German rearmament was only the immediate cause.

How far would the quarrel go? Would it lead to a break in the alliance? Herbert Hoover—like Joseph Kennedy, the former U.S. Ambassador to London—recommended radical measures: It was necessary to "evacuate" Europe and establish a peripheral strategy based on an American "Gibraltar." The formula was seductive, but it did not stand up to close examination. Such a strategy could work only if one disposed of long-range weapons. Without intercontinental rockets, withdrawal to Fortress America would mean the abandonment of Europe to the Soviet Union should she choose to gain control through a combination of military pressure, propaganda, and infiltration. With the Soviet Union mistress of Europe's industrial potential, the balance of power would be changed decisively in her favor, and the United States—isolated, cut off from Africa, pressured by Latin America—would face defeat. The United States, in sum—and this was the contention of the "internationalist" wing of the Republican Party—could not risk a break-up of the Atlantic Pact.

Faced with Soviet messianism, she was no freer to make that political choice than the United States of F.D.R.'s time had been in the face of Nazi Germany's aggression. Europe was a shield. And General Eisenhower (meanwhile appointed Commander in Chief of the North Atlantic Treaty forces) argued another, related point in a speech to the Congress on his return from an inspection trip in Europe: "No matter how strong we prove in keeping open routes of communication, we must always keep open, clearly we must always keep open the areas, keep them open to us when we need their trade in order to exist."* And he concluded by affirming that the "preservation of a free America" required her participation in the defense of Western Europe, and he recommended sending American military units to Europe—this despite the fact that the principal U.S. contribution was supposed to consist of munitions and matériel.

General Eisenhower's support allowed the Administration to carry the day. The "great debate" ended on April 4, 1951, with the passage of a Senate resolution approving the nomination of General Eisenhower as Supreme Allied Commander in Europe and recognizing that "the threat to the security of the United States and our North Atlantic Treaty partners makes it necessary for the United States to station abroad such units of our Armed Forces as may be necessary." The resolution made recommendations on the procedure to be followed and on the guarantees to be obtained from the allies before dispatching troops. The Senate also expressed its feeling that the peace treaty provisions limiting Italy's military strength be modified and that the military resources of West Germany and Spain be more fully utilized.

The United States had originally asked for the participation of the Federal Republic of Germany in Europe's defense, but had obtained nothing more than a French plan for a Euro-

* Report to members of Congress, February 12, 1951.

pean army, which was being considered simultaneously with study of the conditions for German military cooperation. Yet the United States nonetheless accepted the major share of the burden of strengthening Europe's defense. The crisis that might have caused the death of NATO ended by reinforcing the American presence in Europe. After giving economic aid, after joining a regional collective-security system, after deciding to furnish arms, the United States now consented to send her men to protect the European continent. There were some who, observing the logical sequence of these decisions, were ready to see them as an "imperialist" plan for American hegemony in Europe. But, on the contrary, the conditions under which these decisions were made, the passionate debates that accompanied them—in which the most diverse opinions were advanced with a violence all the greater since no one knew where the debate was leading nor what the consequences would be—made it clear that the United States had become involved in spite of herself.

But the strengthening of the military defense of the Atlantic world only partially resolved the problems. There was still no moral unity, no reciprocal confidence, and no agreement on policy among the allies. New crises were to be expected.

{ 5 }

Europe in Crisis: 1952-54

The battle raging across the Atlantic and in the United States in the winter of 1950–51 did not prevent the General Staff of NATO from getting down to work. There could be no waiting for an organized European Defense Community if the Soviet threat was to be met. Yet the strengthening of the NATO structure was not without political consequences, for it shifted the center of gravity in European integration toward the United States. Carrying out the decisions made—whether on the question of establishing an allied high command or of strengthening the armies—once again posed the thorny political problems and technical complications of organizing a coalition with an integrated military force. But the problems were now on a larger scale and infinitely more difficult.

Thus, the problem of creating an infrastructure of bases and depots needed for the projected deployment of troops was tackled. The various bilateral agreements made between the United States and France, Denmark, and Portugal spelled out the conditions for setting up necessary air bases. At the same time, an agreement was reached on the status of soldiers and civilians serving NATO in a country of which they were

not nationals. These agreements, and the progressive establishment of a network of bases, had the effect (greater than
was thought at the time) of binding the allies together. This
infrastructure rooted the Alliance in the soil of each allied
country and gave permanence to a collaboration that had only
just begun.

The reorganization of the NATO Council was undertaken
at the same time. The Defense Committee and Economic and
Finance Committee were integrated into the Council, which
thereby became the only ministerial committee in the whole
organization. From then on, the permanent representatives to
NATO were no longer simply representatives of their foreign
ministers but, rather, of their governments; they became responsible for all questions relating to NATO. This was the
first measure of rationalization, and it was followed by others;
at the Lisbon Conference in 1952, it was decided to regroup
the Secretariat under a Secretary General (whose political
role was soon to surpass his administrative one) and to put
all the NATO offices, including the Council, into Paris.

But these measures of reorganization, although they increased the efficiency of NATO's administrative apparatus,
did not strengthen NATO's authority over the allied countries that had to furnish the money and men. If the United
States was able to honor her commitments, if Canada had the
means to develop its armed forces, most of the other countries
did not, and, in addition, they were faced with other difficulties. The extraordinary rapidity of technical development
meant a constant rise in the price of weapons, which of course
had to be replaced at a greatly accelerated rate. Furthermore,
the steep rise in the cost of raw materials caused by the
Korean War had affected the entire economy. At the Ottowa
Conference held in September, 1951, the delegates in charge
of working on common problems of production and finance
agreed that governmental resistance had seriously hampered
the progress in collaboration. They charged a temporary com-

mittee of three to report on these problems; the committee
was to obtain precise information on defense programs from
each member government, on the exact state of available
troops and equipment, on the cost of defense measures and
their influence on various sectors of the economy, and on the
existing or future measures for the development of the national economies.

Drawing up this over-all picture of government measures
and of the problems to be resolved was considered a quasi-
revolutionary mark of progress on the road to integration.
It was, the committee members noted, the first time that governments of sovereign states had agreed to communicate with
their allies on such "secret" matters, the first time they were
willing to discuss them in common. The temporary committee
insisted on the need for annual reviews, especially for a careful watch over the equitable division of expenses, a "sound
economic and social basis," and a "satisfactory level of general
economic expansion."* It was yet another demonstration of
the fact that military integration implied, almost inevitably, a
certain degree of economic integration. However, the governments that complained that they could not furnish what
was expected of them had to accept the recommendations
made for their military programs and had to be in a position
to act on them. It is true that certain decisions made at the
Lisbon Conference were applied—in particular, those aimed
to adjust the disequilibrium in the balance of payments—but
the military plan calling for 50 divisions and 4,000 airplanes
by the end of 1952 was not to be fulfilled.

Nevertheless, the Lisbon Conference marked a definite stage
in the life of the North Atlantic Treaty Organization. The
period of improvisation and groping was at an end. All the
issues had been put on the table. The road ahead and the
obstacles along the way were now clearly seen. The military,

* Lord Ismay, *NATO: The First Five Years, 1949–54* (Paris, 1955), p. 46.

now free to begin to marshall its forces and to organize the chain of command, breathed a little more easily. General Eisenhower's first annual report ended on an optimistic note: The number of divisions had almost doubled; their combat readiness was improved; their deployment had been examined as a function of the threat from the East; communication systems behind the lines were to be improved.

Moreover, NATO had been strengthened by two new members, Greece and Turkey. Their inclusion in the North Atlantic Pact might seem something of a surprise, and it had, indeed, given rise to much discussion among the allies. It was not because they were sensitive to the evident contradiction in having two Mediterranean countries in an "Atlantic" alliance. Italy's presence had legitimized that of Greece in advance, and everyone had learned long ago to interpret the concept of regionalism loosely. (In fact, anyone who considered the military situation of Europe objectively and who drew up a list of her means of defense could do nothing but opt for NATO.) So the discussions did not center about the question of definition as a matter of principle, but rather about the question of the extended risks implicit in the widening of NATO's zone. Greece and Turkey are located in a particularly exposed area; it was therefore not surprising that the small member states of the Atlantic alliance—Norway and Denmark in particular—felt it difficult to accept allied responsibility for their defense. For the United States, the United Kingdom, and even France—which are, in varying degrees, world powers, and all of which have interests in the Mediterranean—the decision was altogether natural. From the moment the Pact had been signed, the American Government had not disguised the importance it attached to close cooperation with these two guardians of the Mediterranean route, both of which partially protect the lines from the West to the communications and oil centers of the Middle East. The accession of Greece and Turkey satisfied the United States. But, at the same time, it underscored, if there was still need to do so, the priority given to military factors in the concept of the Atlantic alliance. Greece can be considered the cradle of Western civilization, but it was more difficult to legitimize, except by military argument, the inclusion of Turkey in an Atlantic community, even after its "Westernization."

A certain amount of uncertainty did, however, still persist, despite the general satisfaction with the Lisbon proposals for the consolidation of Atlantic institutions. Indeed, in many ways the alliance seemed as fragile as it had at the start.

Europe continued to live in instability. No grave crisis loomed, yet there was no clear improvement in the general economic situation or in political matters. In England, the Conservatives had won the 1951 elections under Churchill's leadership, and thanks to the split in the Labour Party and the support of the petty bourgeoisie had some years before them to keep their promises to revitalize the British economy and revoke the Attlee government's nationalization of the steel and transport industries. For a moment, the impoverished country, refusing to adopt the work pace of its foreign competitors, had to be content with gray austerity.

Nor was there any great change in the balance of political forces in Italy. The economic development of southern Italy was a long-term operation, and, at that point, only relief measures were possible, while attempts were made to evaluate the extent of the problems and to set up an over-all plan. The German Federal Republic, on the other hand, was in full swing. Firmly led by Chancellor Adenauer, who created a political framework for good financial administration, guided by Dr. Erhard along the road to *soziale Marktwirtschaft* (social market economy), benefiting both from the tremendous will to work of the German people, who wished to re-establish a decent standard of living, and from the disarmament that had liberated plant and capital for civilian production, Germany was dominated by the *Wirtschaftswunder* (economic miracle).

In France, the warning signals of a crisis multiplied. The war in Indochina dragged on, its outcome still impossible to foresee, weighing down the French economy and dividing the government, the political parties, and the country itself. Some thought that the French presence on the Indochinese peninsula was necessary if she was to remain a world power. Others, who had popular feeling on their side, thought that the era of colonialism had passed and that it was better to follow the example set by Great Britain in India and Burma than to run the risk of losing everything, as the Netherlands had in Indonesia. But this argument, supported as it was by great good sense, was opposed by those who wanted to continue the war, who pointed to the decision of the U.S.S.R. and the People's Republic of China to recognize Ho Chi Minh's government, and who declared that any agreement with the Vietminh would be a victory for international Communism.

But the Indochinese war had an even more serious effect: By demanding an ever-increasing military effort, it not only kept France from deriving maximum benefits from the Marshall Plan, but, still more, from participating fully in strengthening the forces of NATO. France, thus placed in a false situation vis-à-vis her allies, lost herself in contradictions. Too weak to contribute to her own protection in Europe and at the same time defend her interests in the Far East, she reacted with a display of nationalism that grew stronger in proportion as she became aware of her weakened position. She asked her American ally both to make up for her deficiencies in Europe and to furnish her with the means of remaining in the Far East. Yet she wished to maintain a dominant position on the European continent and exclusive control of operations in Indochina: The internationalization of the Indochinese conflict, which China's support of Ho Chi Minh implied—so the argument ran—legitimized U.S. military and economic aid to a country occupying a key position in Europe, but it did not authorize Washington to interfere in Franco-Vietnamese relations. What France asked was that her American ally admit once and for all that anticolonialism was not the right attitude when faced by the threat of international Communism.

As regards Germany, the creation of the European Defense Community seemed impossible there as well. Not that there was real opposition to reconciliation. On the contrary, the generally favorable reaction to the Schuman Plan had permitted the governments to move rapidly forward; on April 18, 1951, scarcely a year after the project was first suggested, the Treaty setting up the European Coal and Steel Community had been signed. A little more than a year was necessary before the Treaty was ratified and ready to go into effect. On August 10, 1952, the High Authority headed by Jean Monnet took up its functions; this was followed a month later by the first session of the Council of Ministers, and soon, in the first months of 1953, a Common Market for coal, iron ore, and steel was established. This success encouraged attempts for greater coordination in transportation, production and distribution of energy, and agriculture; all with the same goal: to attain integration by passing through and beyond coordination.

On the other hand, the difficult negotiations over the Defense Community once again brought the political problems of integration to the fore; it was clear that the High Authority formula adopted in the ECSC was not applicable to the control of military forces. The constitution of the "Six," which created an entirely new situation for the other European states, forced both members and nonmembers to examine the nature of their relations. Would it be necessary, as Mr. Eden suggested, to reorganize the Council of Europe so that its organs could function as institutions of the European Coal and Steel Community, of the future Defense Community, and of other organizations of the same type and structure? Or was it necessary, as the plan drawn up at the request of the Council of Europe held, to envisage the creation of a European Political Community and to see what its ties to nonmember states and the Council of Europe would be?

The air buzzed with plans and projects, but there was no progress. The two great protagonists, Konrad Adenauer and Robert Schuman, redoubled their efforts to no avail. In vain they demonstrated their willingness to sacrifice sovereignty on the altar of Europe. Resistance was too strong, and the Saar affair hindered them. If it had been up to them alone, a way could have been found to remove one of the obstacles to European integration. But they were both subject to strong pressures. Socialist opposition in Germany was not alone in demanding the return of the Saar; this demand found support among the Free Democrats and even in the Christian Democratic Union. Robert Schuman, for his part, was closely watched by just as vigorous an opposition, in which were found some of the architects of the Franco-Saar economic and customs union.

The question of the Saar played only a secondary role, however, and the "Saar first" demand (settlement of the Saar question as a precondition for further negotiation), formulated by René Mayer at the beginning of 1953, was only a domestic political maneuver. The fundamental quarrel was over the European Defense Community. This—added to all the other factors that make for divisiveness among a people of retentive memory who are disposed toward abstract discussion of principles—was the issue that was to render France almost ungovernable. In order to avoid German rearmament within the framework of the Atlantic Pact, the French Government had proposed the formation of a European army. Its insistence had been so strong that the State Department and the President of the United States were won over to its point of view (despite the skepticism of the Department of Defense), and it also obtained the agreement of the NATO Council. At the

Lisbon Conference, the Council, though not without some trouble, finally came out in favor of the plan for a European Defense Community. It was signed at the beginning of May, 1952, by the six interested states.

But the French Parliament still had to be convinced of the validity of this solution. Resistance was strong, and it was increasing. Criticism of the Treaty focused first of all on the abstention of Great Britain, which left France alone vis-à-vis Germany. But it was aimed equally at German rearmament, the principal objective of the Treaty and its clauses—clauses that were, moreover, analogous to those in the ECSC Treaty in that they implied a sacrifice of sovereignty for supranational institutions. What had appeared tolerable so long as it was only a question of coal and steel became inadmissible the moment it was applied to military matters.

The Treaty thus reflected the climate in which it had been drawn up, the hopes and fears of its authors—their desire to create a united Europe, but also their persistent fear of Germany. But the precautions against Germany inevitably hindered the freedom of movement of the other contracting parties as well. They had wished to avoid the reconstitution of a German national army; but the same clauses that applied to one applied to the other, and at one blow the French, Italian, Belgian, and Dutch governments were also deprived of the freedom to dispose of their national forces. For this reason, the Treaty was attacked from all sides for its textual imprecisions as well as for more fundamental reasons. An opposition coalition, rather loosely knit to be sure, was formed. It was made up of Communists (who, despite their isolation, represented a certain strength), and the classic right wing, joined by the Gaullists, some radicals, and socialists. Political parties in favor of the Treaty were for the most part divided, and the government did not dare fight back. It was not until January, 1953, that the Treaty was submitted to the Parliament for ratification. Eight months had gone by, a lapse of time from which the opponents of the Defense Community had greatly benefited.

Meanwhile, changes had taken place in the United States. The Democratic Administration had used all its resources in the fight to win the "great debate" over Europe and the simultaneous battle over General MacArthur and its China policy. From then on, it had been unable to move from the defensive to which it had been forced by furious Republican attackers, who felt their hour of revenge had come at last. Indeed, what arguments *could* it present against opponents who charged it with failure of its foreign policy? That American intervention in Greece and Turkey, the Marshall Plan, the Berlin Airlift, and the Korean engagement had stopped Soviet advances? This was undoubtedly true. But how many hopes had *not* been realized! How many promises had *not* been kept! A United States of Europe beginning to take shape after four years of economic aid was probably like the mirages seen by parched travelers in the desert. China was lost. The Korean War was dragging on endlessly. All that money, generously and intelligently distributed as it was, seemed to have been thrown into a bottomless well. The Americans were alone. No matter what they did, criticism rained down from all sides, giving way to flattery only when money was needed.

The Republicans had all the advantages: They could point to Yalta and the errors committed in interpreting Soviet policy; they did not fail to exploit the Hiss case to show how far the government had allowed itself to be infiltrated by Communists. As remarkable a President as Harry Truman may have been, he could not help but be the target for these jeers. His immediate associates were open to attack, and attacked they were. Certain scandals implicating members of the Administration were immediately exploited to the full. The conservative South, where Harry Truman had determined opponents— James Byrnes among them—had opposed not only the Fair

Deal, but also all the increased expenditures due to "big government" and the increase in international responsibilities.

In brief, the feeling spread during 1952 that the Democrats' days were numbered. Once it was sure that President Truman would retire, and once the candidates, General Eisenhower and Adlai Stevenson, had been nominated, the Administration's potential for action was reduced and its influence in Europe diminished. This American governmental crisis—not too strong a term for the political vacuum created by the opening of the electoral campaign—came at the least opportune moment. Vigorous complementary action on both sides of the Atlantic in 1952 would have been able to bring about a decision in favor of the European Defense Community. By 1953, it was too late.

General Eisenhower's victory, however, gave rise to great hopes in Europe as well as in the United States. They were legitimate, if one recalls all the opportunities open to him. Elected by an almost plebiscitary vote to the head of a Presidential democracy, he had enormous powers. Behind him stood a public that would allow him to make momentous decisions. His Atlantic allies were ready to put their trust in him. There was a feeling of gratitude toward this man who twice had been their commander-in-chief and who had been popular everywhere he went. The crucial part he had played in sending American troops to Europe was well known. But it was also believed that the General was a man of peaceful temperament, and that he was a politician more than a soldier.

The beginning seemed encouraging. The new President "barricaded himself among honest men," all of whom shared a reputation for moderation. There were no reactionaries or neo-isolationists in his Cabinet. The new Administration, it was thought, would be moderately conservative yet willing to take up liberal positions—on the Negro problem, for instance. The differences between this and the preceding Presidency would be more of style than of principle.

But a certain disappointment became apparent rather quickly. America expected its President to be an activist. It was from him that the initiative was supposed to come. It was up to him and him alone to show the way. A President both reigns and governs; for the man at the head of the strongest nation on earth, it is a crushing burden. The President now sought "to get out from under." He acted by delegating his powers, like an army commander who counts on his chief of staff to co-ordinate the activity of the troops. The formula is not a bad one inasmuch as it allows both distance and time for reflection. But it is efficient only if the objective has been previously defined and the line of action indicated. From the very first month, however, the feeling grew that the leadership was not as strong as this system of governing requires. The President seemed to allow the Congress the widest use of its preroga-tives. He did not take in hand and organize that party that had brought him to power. His behavior was more that of an arbiter than of a leader.

This method of government was surprising, if not com-pletely confusing. It did not correspond to the accepted con-cept of Presidential power, modifying as it did the respective roles of the Presidency and the Congress and giving the legis-lators great freedom of movement—which some were not slow to abuse. This weakening of Presidential power was all the more dangerous since the Republican Party was divided and the "internationalists" of the White House were unable to set the tone in either the House of Representatives or the Senate. Robert Taft was still, despite his differences of opinion on some policies, of great value to the White House. But what of a Jenner or a McCarthy? The President's silence or reserve allowed McCarthy and his followers to dominate the political scene for some months and to undertake, by most questionable means, a hunt for Communists that was transformed into a hunt for intellectual and for civil servants guilty of having served in the Democratic Administration.

This phase of the exploitation of the Republican electoral victory had most unfortunate effects. It turned away a great number of extremely valuable men from public service, most particularly from diplomatic service. It was the first blow to President Eisenhower's prestige; his silence on the issue was interpreted rather as a manifestation of weakness than as the expression of some tactical plan. It was difficult to understand or excuse the fact why certain cases of injustice and injury had not been rectified. Moreover, the President's silence encouraged cowardice at the lower levels of government—a demoralizing factor. Finally, the McCarthyite wave made the most deplorable impression throughout the world and, at a moment that was particularly important for the new Administration, furnished effective arguments for the numerous critics of American policy. Indeed, McCarthyism supplied the Communists with a needed proof of their argument that anti-Communism inevitably leads to fascism.

But that was not the only cause of surprise and disappointment. The new Administration sought to revive the dynamism American foreign policy had lost. It did not succeed and, instead, allowed itself to be caught in a web of contradictions. The announced intention to substitute "roll-back" for "containment" had aroused as much hope as anxiety; that was why, at the moment of Stalin's death, when the Soviet regime was shaken and torn by various movements, and especially after the East Berlin riots on June 17, 1954, some kind of American initiative was expected. But nothing happened. From Washington came counsels of prudence, dictated by good sense, perhaps, but nonetheless appearing to contradict the declarations Eisenhower had made in the course of his campaign. The policies in Korea and Formosa were equally surprising. Why did the United States disengage herself in Korea, where she was responding in the name of the United Nations to an aggression that clearly demanded the application of the principle of collective security, only to stand firm in Formosa

behind a regime that had scarcely any future? And why give
Chiang Kai-shek a freedom of action that he could use only
with American support, and at the same time carry on negotiations at Panmunjom? This transfer of American effort from
the Korean peninsula to the island of Formosa was justified,
perhaps, by strategic arguments or the dictates of domestic
politics, but it was not understood by the allies of the United
States, Great Britain in particular.

Last but not least, U.S. Soviet policy slowly evolved in a
way that was bound to have repercussions on her relations
with the Atlantic allies. The policy of the Democratic Administration had made ideology a major factor in the explanation
of Soviet behavior: The U.S.S.R. followed the policy of a
revolutionary power; she was impelled at the same time by a
Russian and a Soviet messianism; and the instruments she used
to reach her goals were as much of an ideological and political
as of a military nature. John Foster Dulles, however, was of
the opinion that Soviet Russia practiced classic power politics.
Although aware of the effects of subversive activities, he was
apt to consider the role of armies more important. Whereas
his predecessors had attached great importance to the political
aspect of the Soviet threat, he emphasized its military implications. Furthermore, the Korean experience led him to investigate the possibility of avoiding a show of force on terrain
chosen by the enemy; instead, he wished to learn how to
impose the terrain and arms of one's own choosing on the
enemy. It was with these considerations in mind that he came
to formulate his concept of "massive retaliation."

This highlighting of the military character of the war provoked increased criticisms and reservations in Europe concerning American policy, especially when considered together
with American declarations on "roll-back" and massive retaliation. This "dynamism," far from imparting courage to the
Atlantic allies, only alarmed them, and increased rather than
diminished the number of opponents to the European Defense

Community. In December, 1953, when John Foster Dulles told the French in no uncertain terms that it was time to end their dilatory maneuvers, and when he hurled at them the threat of an "agonizing reappraisal" of American foreign policy, emotion and irritation reached their height.

This ultimatum was, no doubt, helpful insofar as it clarified the situation. But at the same time it revealed the depth of disagreement between France and the United States.

That there was such disagreement is hardly surprising. By the beginning of 1954, the combination of the Indochinese war and the quarrel over the European Defense Community had created a truly explosive situation in France. The government knew, in fact, that there was no longer a majority supporting either the Indochinese war or the ratification of the EDC treaty. But it did not want to admit this, and it could not do so without having all its supporters unite against it and thus lose the majority that kept it in power.

For a moment, it seemed that the situation in Indochina could still be saved. Faced with evidence of Chinese intervention, the American Government considered the next step. Was not the total loss of the Indochinese peninsula too dangerous even to contemplate? The country was rich and of undeniable strategic importance for any nation wishing to control Southeast Asia. Some of President Eisenhower's advisers pressed him to intervene. He was ready to do so, but chose finally to abstain from action. American intervention would risk a broadening of the Indochinese conflict, for which the President did not wish to assume responsibility. There was no alternative but to negotiate, and negotiate under the worst possible conditions, since Dien Bien Phu fell while the Asian Conference was meeting at Geneva to negotiate the peace in Indochina. For France, the humiliation was cruel, so cruel that it finally brought about the eruption of the crisis that everyone had feared. And thus Mendès-France came to power.

Pierre Mendès-France had been waiting for this moment

for a long time, and many had been waiting with him. On the postwar French political scene, he was one of the few persons who showed the characteristics of a real statesman, who from the beginning gave the impression of knowing what he wanted and of having a definite policy. Yet he was feared for these very qualities, and his single-mindedness made enemies: He was accused of being too personal to play the parliamentary game and collaborate on a governmental team. Mendès-France did not stand alone, however. He had his admirers and, like all politicians of a certain kind, a following. He had some solid support in the Radical Party, and in the Socialist Party and in leftist circles he was looked on as the one man capable of uniting the French left.

What would he do? What could he do? Nothing but attend to the most pressing things first. Negotiations were under way in Geneva: Mendès-France was convinced the conference must permit France to disengage herself from a debilitating war; he did not hesitate publicly to set himself a time limit within which, as he promised, he would effect this solution. It was a diplomatic success obtained at the price of abandoning a French position. But in France, the majority of the public was grateful to him for having ended the whole venture.

France was in check elsewhere as well. It was necessary to normalize relations with Tunisia. Again, Mendès-France did not hesitate to make the necessary concessions. Then, the turn of the European Defense Community came. A new postponement seemed neither possible nor desirable. The moment of decision had come. And it came, without debate, on a simple parliamentary motion: The Assembly refused to consider the ratification of the Treaty. The government had not even made its preferences known.

All over Europe there was consternation. The allies were obviously annoyed. The Bonn Government, which had put everything it had behind its effort to obtain ratification of the EDC, was not pleased at being exposed to the opposition's taunts and sarcasm. In Belgium and Holland, where actual constitutional modifications had been made to permit ratification, the anger and mortification were extreme. The Italians, who had prudently waited for the French decision before acting themselves, were less annoyed, but like everyone else were somewhat disturbed. Was the rejection of the European Defense Community to be the first step leading to the breakdown and reversal of alliances?

This widespread anxiety, however, was the result of a rather hasty analysis of the situation and an overly pessimistic interpretation of Mendès-France's political intentions. His opponents accused him of secret collusion with the Communists and of preparing a new popular front that would adopt "neutralist" policies in foreign affairs. But the head of the government, independent as he may have been and despite his decision to break with the methods of his predecessors, had only limited freedom of action. To break with the Atlantic Pact would be to involve France in a dangerous new adventure, to threaten the entire system built up since 1948 both in Europe and across the Atlantic, and raise anew the issue of the German Federal Republic without any benefit for France. As for the economic consequences of a rupture of Atlantic ties, Mendès-France could appreciate them better than anyone, for he could gauge the sacrifices that such a reversal of present economic trends would require. There was certainly no majority support in France for such a policy.

In any event, the rejection of the European Defense Community did not automatically imply the break-up of the Atlantic Alliance. On the contrary, the existence of NATO offered the possibility of a substitute solution, the very one that had been refused in 1950. Mendès-France thus sought a way out of the crisis with a formula that would quiet all the various opposition that had defeated the EDC. The Brussels Treaty would be the basis on which he could found a new Union of Western Europe. This plan had the double advantage of assuring the participation of the United Kingdom in the Continental defense and of not forcing the signatories to abandon sovereign rights for supranational institutions. The negotiations on the matter were lively and vigorous; they ended, on October 23, 1954, with the signing of the Paris Agreements, which was ratified six months later.

Finally, then, after the long and dramatic crisis, the Federal Republic of Germany suddenly found herself in a Western European Union, and as a member of a group of signatory states of the Brussels Treaty, which could easily have been interpreted as a pact directed against her. The relentless opposition of the Soviet Union to the reunification of Germany on any but her own terms had finally forced the Western governments to a choice they had wished to avoid. There was nothing more significant than Article 2 of Protocol No. 1 of the Brussels Treaty: "The sub-paragraph of the Preamble to the Treaty: 'to take such steps as may be held necessary in the event of renewal by Germany of a policy of aggression' shall be modified to read: 'to promote the unity and to encourage the progressive integration of Europe.'"

But this new importance of the Brussels Treaty did not imply, as one might imagine, a strengthening of the Western European Union and a success for the "Europeans." Article 3 of Protocol No. 1 of the Brussels Treaty stated:

> The following new Article shall be inserted in the Treaty as Article 4: "In the execution of the Treaty the High Contracting Parties and any organs established by Them under the Treaty shall work in close co-operation with the North Atlantic Treaty Organization.
>
> "Recognizing the undesirability of duplicating the Military Staffs of NATO, the Council and its agency will rely on the appropriate Military Authorities of NATO for information and advice on military matters."*

* Protocol modifying and completing the Brussels Treaty, Paris, October 23, 1954, in "Treaty Series No. 39," 1955 (London: H. M. Stationery Office, 1955).

The Federal Republic of Germany thus became, contrary to every expectation, a member of NATO. Naturally, there were certain specific conditions of her entry: abstention from any action incompatible with the strictly defensive nature of the two treaties; renunciation of the use of force to obtain Germany's reunification or the modification of her frontiers. But in exchange, Germany obtained the abrogation of her occupied status as well as full sovereign status over her internal and external affairs. Was this victory of Chancellor Adenauer, this equality of rights he had so long demanded, acquired at the expense of Europe? At first glance, it did indeed appear so. There were many who thought—one has only to read the press comments on the Paris Agreements to see this—that the failure of the European Defense Community meant the definitive end to the movement for European integration. "The idea of a federal organization for the 'Europe of the six' is dead," wrote one, after noting that the failure was that of the "European" party, a failure from which it had not recovered. But this judgment was somewhat too categorical. If it was true that the rejection of the European Defense Community was the expression of a refusal to opt for supranational solutions, one could not necessarily conclude that it was a victory of "neutralists" over "Europeans," or even that it would permanently transfer the focal point of integration efforts toward the Atlantic. The existence of the North Atlantic Pact offered a substitute solution to those who wanted neither a European tête-à-tête with a rearmed Germany nor the risk of seeing Germany turn toward the Soviet Union. In this constant oscillation between Europe and the Atlantic Community, the latter had momentarily carried the day, not so much because of what the Americans wanted, or because of pressure or intervention on their part, but because of the single fact of American power and French impotence. For American power, the "Europeans" could offer no valid practical substitute. That the French Premier Mendès-France should have been the prime mover behind the crisis and the *dénouement* as well demonstrates clearly enough the decisive influence of a simple relationship of forces.

{ 6 }

Suez and Budapest

As one might imagine, the Soviet Union had carefully followed the ups and downs of the battle over EDC. And of course, she had not hesitated to make her opinion known publicly, endlessly denouncing the German and French "warmongers" and *revanchistes* in order to give moral support to those in France who for one reason or another were opposed to German rearmament. She was delighted with the vote in the National Assembly, on August 30, 1954—a "victory for peace."

The conclusion of the Paris Agreements therefore was an acute disappointment for Russia. The resultant strengthening of the Western position would force her to reappraise the situation. The new conclusions arrived at by the Soviet leaders —in the course of discussions about which, as always, we know nothing—were manifested in two different decisions. First, they set up a military organization grouping the states of Eastern Europe around the Soviet Union as a counterpart to the NATO now strengthened by the Federal Republic of Germany: This was the Warsaw Pact, signed in May, 1955, and conceived as a defensive alliance made necessary by the threat of German rearmament. But this stiffening in the military arena was accompanied by a new flexibility in the area of diplomacy. Nikita Khrushchev and Nikolai Bulganin, his colleague of the moment, went off on a series of trips that at one and the same time demonstrated the desire of the Soviet Government to emerge from its isolation and bore witness to its pacific intentions.

Austria was the first to benefit from the Soviet Union's attention. The last obstacles to the independence promised her in 1943 melted away, and on May 15, 1955, the state treaty was signed. Austria recovered her sovereignty, proclaimed her neutrality, and obtained admission to the United Nations and the Council of Europe. The new state came out of its terrible trials stronger than it had been for a long time past. It was more assured and balanced economically, politically, and spiritually. Austria had accepted the fact that she was a small nation. She had absorbed the shock of her "Marignan," and the younger generation, far from taking pleasure, as had their elders between the wars, in the evocation of past glories, dreamed of living far removed from great adventure. The memory of the Soviet occupation—and the awareness of the geographical proximity of a regime for which the Austrians, who had some experience of it, had no taste—encouraged prudence. Despite the difficulties inherent in any coalition government, the Socialist and the People's parties, the two major groupings, were wise enough to preserve a regime of national union.

But the Soviet leaders were not satisfied with this single demonstration of their good will. They also traveled to Belgrade, undertook negotiations for a peace treaty with Japan, and invited Chancellor Adenauer to Moscow with a view to establishing diplomatic relations between the U.S.S.R. and the Federal Republic. The Summit Conference of July, 1955, at Geneva seemed to herald a thaw in the Cold War. Khrushchev and Bulganin pursued their campaign, multiplied their meet-

ings and trips, sought to establish better contacts everywhere
—never, however, neglecting an occasion to reaffirm their
faith in Marxism-Leninism and their conviction that Communism would one day defeat capitalism. But in fact, it was
less that still far-off future which occupied them than a more
immediate aim: the liquidation of Stalin's heritage.

The operation implied certain risks. In a regime that had
been built on the dogma of the leader's infallibility, in which
the leader alone had the right to establish valid interpretations
of the Marxist texts, any questioning of the policies of a man
who for almost twenty-three years had reigned over all could
not fail to shake the very foundations of his successors' power.
At the Twentieth Congress of the Communist Party of the
Soviet Union, Nikita Khrushchev opened a breach in the
Soviet edifice that was to widen further in the months to come
and even jeopardize its very existence.

The relaxation of Soviet pressure did create a somewhat
easier atmosphere on both sides of the Atlantic. No great conflicts disturbed international relations, and everyone attentively followed the Soviet "peace offensive," which, according to one's temperament and how much information one had,
either awakened hope or encouraged skepticism. The allied
governments, close as their official contacts were, were far
from agreement on certain basic problems, and public opinion
in each country varied radically on all of them. In Europe, the
contradictions in U.S. economic policy were remarked on,
particularly the concessions the President thought he had to
make to protectionists, which seemed astonishing in view of
the repeated advice to the contrary from men close to him
who, like himself, were "internationalist" Republicans. There
was continued coolness toward John Foster Dulles; he was respected, but he did not arouse sympathy. Both because of his
temperament and the circumstances in which he worked, he
seemed more like a government official than a diplomat. In the

formulation of American foreign policy, he played, in fact, the role the President refused to assume. He had to define, to order, to speak loud and clear, whereas his job should have been simply the conduct of negotiations. This basic contradiction, which became even more apparent after General Eisenhower's illness, complicated his task. It exposed him to criticism and provoked grave distrust among his fellow negotiators, who could not discover what his real intentions were. This personal difficulty was compounded by the disagreement among the allies as to the nature of the Soviet threat, a difference of opinion only sharpened by the flexibility of Soviet policy. Dulles's obstinate emphasis on the Soviet military threat was matched by his colleagues' insistence on the importance of economic competition and political warfare.

But above all, the differences in the political climate on each side of the Atlantic complicated relations among the allies. As tense as relations may have been at certain moments between the Labour Party in England and Truman's Administration in America, there had been more contact and possibility for agreement between them than now existed between the Conservative Government and the Republican Administration. The differences between Truman's liberalism and Attlee's Labour policy were perhaps less great than those between Butler's social liberalism and the economic policies of a Republican Party whose financial orthodoxy was matched by narrowness of outlook and in which professions of faith in free enterprise were accompanied by persistent protectionist practice. Paradoxical as it may be, the Republicans—a party whose leaders are recruited from among those American circles that are supposed to have the most international "contacts"—gave the impression of knowing and understanding Europe even less than their Democratic predecessors. The result was, of course, constant misunderstanding and *malaise*. The European left, moreover, never missed a chance to show its opposition to a Republican Party it considered re-

actionary. When the Labour Party moved to the Opposition
benches, relieved of the burdens of power, its policies and
attitude immediately hardened, only complicating the job
faced by the Conservative Government. In France and Italy,
nothing happened to change the continuing lack of enthusiasm over the American ally. The government officials saw to
it that necessary and useful contacts were maintained, but public opinion was still fairly critical—the Communists very much
so, until the Twentieth Congress forced them into a preoccu-
pation with their own internal affairs. It was only with the
Federal Republic of Germany that United States relations
could be considered excellent. This was no doubt due to personal contacts, to the reciprocal esteem of the two policy-
makers, Eisenhower and Adenauer, and to certain tempera-
mental affinities. But it was due equally to the success of the
German economic experiment. Germany had regained confidence in herself and thus gained the confidence of the United
States—and the confidence of France, as well. With the end
of the quarrel over EDC and the conclusion of the Paris
Agreements, the heavy burden weighing on Franco-German
relations lifted. The rejection by the Saarlanders (in the referendum of 1955) of the European status offered them, far from
provoking a new crisis, on the contrary opened the way to a
settlement that was to eliminate the last cause of tension between France and Germany. In Paris, the government and
parliament bowed to a decision against which appeal was difficult. The French public scarcely reacted at all; it had never
been very concerned over the Saar. In Germany, the general
popular satisfaction over the vote permitted the government
a certain magnanimity in the final negotiations over the transfer of the Saar from one regime to another. From then on, the
reconciliation of the two countries, for so long set against each
other in apparently eternal antagonism, appeared complete.
Both seemed convinced of the need for close collaboration in

economic and political affairs, and convinced as well of the interpenetration of their interests.

The benefit derived by Europe as a whole from this Franco-German *rapprochement* more than compensated for the failure of EDC and the Saar referendum. The nationalist feelings that had been set against the establishment of supranational institutions were not disturbed by the kind of effective cooperation now being organized.

Those people who, preoccupied with the Soviet Union, had allowed themselves to be persuaded of the hope of a thaw in the Cold War, were now to be brutally reminded that the history of the world in the twentieth century was not merely that of a dialogue between the Soviet empire and the United States and her allies. The rise of Asian and African nationalism, and revolutions of the peoples still subjugated by imperialist systems, placed Europe, and more especially the members of the Atlantic Alliance, in a new and difficult position.

In the Mediterranean, the pace quickened noticeably. The United Kingdom, alone in the Middle East after the departure of the French, was forced to abandon the positions she held there, retreating before the tide of an Arab nationalism given renewed momentum by Colonel Nasser's leadership. She punctiliously observed the clauses of the treaty of October, 1954, stipulating the evacuation of the Suez bases and the return of the installations to the Egyptians. On June 13, 1956, the last British soldier departed, and Egypt regained full independence. But Great Britain had no luck. The unfortunate effects of losing the Egyptian bases, which had allowed her to control the access routes to the Middle East and also to keep open the road to the Indian Ocean, could have been mitigated by the use of other bases in either the Arabian Peninsula, Jordan, Iraq, or Cyprus. But at this very moment, the conflict over Cyprus, which had been simmering for years, entered a more acute phase. What the Cypriots wanted was full independ-

ence, which, for the majority of them, was considered the
first step on the way to union with Greece. The conflict was
all the more serious in that it involved three allies in the
Atlantic Pact and for several years placed Greece and Turkey
in implacable opposition, thereby weakening one of the most
vulnerable flanks of the Alliance.

France was also having difficulties. The Mahgreb wanted its
independence. Concessions made in Tunisia—which were followed by Bourguiba's return and the recognition of an independent Tunisia in interdependent relation to France—led to
the demand for similar measures in Morocco. But more time
was necessary before taking the first step in Morocco, for the
groups in opposition there were more powerful and more
committed. The deposition of Sultan Sidi ben-Youssef had
contributed to the hardening of the respective positions. It
was only in 1955 that the French Government agreed to make
the decisive gesture. The return of Sidi ben-Youssef at the
beginning of November of the same year was followed by
an agreement incorporating the Tunisian formula of independence and interdependence.

In Algeria, revolt broke out early in November, 1954.
There, the problem was more difficult. Algeria was part of
Metropolitan France. It was considered to be French territory, inhabited by a European population (substantially larger
than that in either Tunisia or Morocco) that considered Algeria its home. But the rebels were organized, tough, and
tenacious, and their guerrilla tactics, given the local conditions
of Algeria's terrain and population, were singularly effective.
France was therefore forced to send an increasing number of
troops to Algeria, which prevented her from adequately supplying her European front. The Indochinese drama was re-
peating itself.

These Mediterranean complications put NATO into a delicate position. From all indications, its most important task
was to resolve the Cyprus problem. But the efforts to mediate

were strongly resisted by both parties. As for the Algerian crisis, it was all the more dangerous, for it compromised French relations with Tunisia and Morocco, where American NATO bases were located. What is more, the "French Departments of Algeria" were expressly included in the territory covered by the Atlantic security system. If the conflict were prolonged—which could very well mean that it would also extend geographically and intensify politically—the Atlantic allies would be faced with grave decisions, all the harder to make in that it was so difficult to understand the problem France confronted.

The question was far bigger than the Algerian framework in which it was posed. It was first of all a question of whether world powers bound together in a regional pact could keep their freedom of action outside the region of that alliance. The Government of the United States, concerned with Latin America, Asia, Africa, and the ever stronger tide of nationalism, did not wish to be or appear to be tugged along in Europe's wake. And this desire to maintain independence of action was strengthened by the old anticolonialist traditions of the American people. Why support policies one disapproves of, and thus be cut off from peoples who, if not supported in the United States, would undoubtedly turn to the Soviet Union or China? On the contrary, by maintaining ties with the new states and with peoples seeking independence, the United States could contribute to the containment of the Communist advances and to the protection of Europe. For John Foster Dulles, there was no contradiction between U.S. participation in NATO and her support of or sympathy for the peoples seeking independence from colonial imperialism.

It was thus not surprising that President Nasser's announcement of the nationalization of the Universal Company of the Suez Canal put the Atlantic allies, and especially the three chiefly concerned, into an enormously difficult situation. The action could have been predicted, and it had been prepared for in minute detail. But it sowed disorder nonetheless. President Nasser announced it as a move against colonial powers. The argument was scarcely valid, but it had its effect in the United States, where the name of the Suez Company did not have the power to evoke the memories it did in Europe. The different points of view emerged at once: The English and the French were reunited in the face of a unilateral breaking off of a contract, a deliberately calculated provocation; the American Government was more reserved. Dulles reassured his countrymen on his return from the first London Conference: The United States had made no commitments. The affair dragged on and the possibilities for an effective reply to Nasser's action grew fewer. France and England were enormously irritated with their American ally. There was a feeling of having been dropped, and Dulles was attacked for an offhandedness all the more annoying since his treatment of the Aswan Dam question had contributed to the outbreak of the crisis in the first place.

It was under these conditions that the double crisis of the autumn of 1956 burst forth.

On October 23, several thousand students in Budapest assembled at the monument to the Polish general Bem, the hero of the Hungarian Revolution of 1848. With this symbolic homage, they intended to show their opposition to the police state and foreign domination. There was nothing in their demands that had not already been expressed in previous months by them, by the intellectuals, by the spokesmen for the peasants and workers, or by their Polish neighbors. They did not demand that the regime be liquidated, only that it be relaxed. Like the Poles, they put their trust in a Communist, Imre Nagy. And, as in Poland, the departure of the Soviet troops was a condition for the restoration of their freedom.

The October 23 demonstration was bigger than previous ones and aroused an enthusiasm that the resistance of the authorities only amplified. A crowd then gathered in front of the radio station, and the spokesmen for the demonstrators asked to be allowed to broadcast their messages. At that moment, the first shots were fired. These were the shots that transformed a simple appeal into revolution. Soviet troops could do nothing against so formidable a mass movement. The Hungarian people had risen, forcing concession after concession from those who sought to lead them. On October 29, the Revolution appeared victorious: The imminent withdrawal of Soviet troops was announced.

But on this same October 29, there was other news. Israel had decided to take action against Egypt. The Israeli attack was followed the next day by a Franco-British ultimatum to Israel and its Egyptian enemy: They had twelve hours to establish a cease-fire, or the Suez Canal would be occupied. All at once, the world faced two crises, either of which could lead to a general conflict. Neither had been entirely unexpected.

The reactions in the Soviet Union and the satellite countries to the death of Stalin, and particularly to the re-examination of his regime by his successors, were well known in the West. After hearing the leaders of the satellite countries indulge in public self-criticism, it was impossible to ignore the fact that a double opposition, both nationalist and social, was developing in the Soviet world. The seriousness of the conflicts dividing the Middle East—where Egypt, as leader of a more or less united Arab coalition, was fighting two battles at once, one against Israel, the other against France and Great Britain—had also been known.

The surprise was nonetheless total. And it can only be explained by the suddenness of the crises and by their unexpectedly explosive character, as well as by the extreme rapidity of events. It was all the more difficult to grasp this rapid pace when one was intellectually so poorly prepared to understand it, accustomed as one was to the soothing clichés fostered by the relaxed international climate. In a world that was periodically stunned with terrifying revelations on the development of nuclear weapons, no one believed that war was still possible; no nation would deliberately assume such a responsibility. History, it is true, furnishes more than one example of these terrible webs of circumstance in which men and nations find themselves caught. But the lessons of history were scarcely heeded. What was still more disconcerting was the simultaneity of the two crises and the conditions in which they had arisen.

In Hungary, the regime fell victim to the very people on whom it had most depended, the intellectuals, the students, and the workers. To the intellectuals, the regime had offered money and honors. To the young, it had been preaching for ten years that the future lay in the framework of Marxism. As for the workers, the proletariat in whose name the regime governed, in theory were they not the masters? Yet all of these rose against the government and struck a mortal blow to the myth of totalitarianism's invincibility. Until then, it had been thought that a totalitarian regime, because of its propaganda and police, was too strong to be defeated from within. But the Hungarian Revolution showed that neither police nor propaganda can give roots to a system that survives only by virtue of outside support.

In the Middle East, three quarrels were being settled at the same time: that of Israel against an Egypt intent on working for her destruction; that of France against an Egypt supporting the revolt of North Africa; and that of Great Britain against an Egypt that threatened her by the nationalization of the Suez Company. All the resentments against President Nasser were now being aired at once. But the reasons for such resentment did not coincide. The presence of a common adversary had created an alliance that did not wish to be one, and led to a war in everything but name. Israel had no other objective than the destruction of Egyptian bases from which the "volunteers of death" carried out their raids. As for France and Britain, they intervened only to separate the belligerents, but in a location that revealed their other intentions. And the manner in which this intervention was prepared, announced, and carried out only aggravated the confusion and made an explanation of it more difficult. If surprise is what France and Britain were after, they had fully succeeded.

Great Britain, as her leaders had never failed to proclaim since the war, founded her policy on three basic points: the Commonwealth, the American alliance, and the United Nations. In this instance, the British Government warned neither her allies nor the United Nations. Together with France, it had moved without psychological preparation or diplomatic consultation—an enormous risk not so much because of the dimensions of the immediate problem, but because it brought into question the very basis of British policy.

The intensity of the Soviet Union's reaction against the uprising in Hungary and against Franco-British and Israeli troops was as great a surprise as the two original crises. In Western Europe, public opinion followed the Hungarian struggle for freedom with the passion of those who know their own future is at stake. But the rest of the world, for whom Hungary was a peripheral problem, turned to the Middle East, and it was there that all interests converged. For the Asian nations, the Franco-British intervention was a perfect demonstration of colonial imperialism, a policy from which they themselves had been liberated too recently not to respond with a collective-defense reflex. For the Soviet Union—which, after long preparation, had acquired allies and certain key positions in the Middle East—it was a perfect opportunity to strengthen her influence and tighten the bonds between Arab nationalism and Communism. She promised to rush to the aid of the Arab nations.

As for the American Administration, forced by its allies (in

the midst of an election campaign) to make a choice it had
always tried to avoid, and indignant at the idea that it was
being maneuvered by them, it took a position no doubt different from that which obtained in government circles in
London or Paris. How was it to legitimize support for a
colonialist policy of which it disapproved when there was
always the threat that the Asian and African world would
turn increasingly to the Soviet Union as the only possible
protector against European imperialism, especially when
France and Great Britain were flouting the United Nations
and endangering the existence of that institution so necessary
to world peace?

Moreover, the United States had interests in the Middle
East that were too important to allow her to remain indifferent
to Franco-British action. To what extent were these interests
involved? What was the attitude of the great oil companies?
What weight did they have in State Department deliberations?
Nothing was more difficult to say. Those who attributed a
dominating, if not determining, influence to economic factors
thought they could prove that the oil interests were of decisive
importance. But this thesis was based on no verified or veri-
fiable fact. That the government took oil interests into account
is absolutely certain, particularly since Under Secretary
Hoover, who, in the absence of Dulles, had the principal responsibility, was an expert on oil. But it is quite another thing
to imagine that he went so far as to subordinate the national
interest to the interest of a small, albeit powerful, group in a
decision affecting U.S. policy. Moreover, the President himself
played a decisive role. He was forced by his allies to acknowl-
edge a *fait accompli* that, if he consented in it, would make
him their accomplice in war at the very moment he was presenting himself to the American people as the defender of
peace. He could not hesitate. His support went to the United
Nations.

Thus confronted with a heterogeneous but slowly organizing coalition against them, the three governments had to give way. Isolated in the United Nations, threatened by the Soviet Union with military intervention, pressured by the United States, they were forced to call a cease-fire. What is more, the British Government had seen the majority of the British people—or those who claimed to speak for them—unite in violent opposition to the Suez expedition. Eden did not dare to assume sole responsibility for completing a common undertaking.

Despite the incontestable military victory of the Israeli troops, it was a major political defeat all around. The failure of the Suez expedition showed to all the world the limits of French and British power and the degree of their dependence on the United States. Still more serious was the blow struck to the prestige of European and Atlantic solidarity. In siding with the Asian and Arab states, the United States had undoubtedly aroused sympathies from which the West would indirectly benefit. But this alone would not resolve the problems created by the change in relations between Europe and other continents. Anticolonialism is not a policy in itself, especially—and this is the case in certain countries—if it masks an aggressive and conquering nationalism. By persisting in its desire to limit geographically the obligations it assumed in the Atlantic Pact, the American Government arrived at an impasse. First of all, this geographical limitation was open to question: The NATO zone included Greece and Turkey, after all—that is to say, the eastern basin of the Mediterranean. Secondly, and more important, the United States' principal allies in Europe had world obligations, and any weakening of their world position automatically implied a weakening of NATO.

The double crisis of November also underlined the weakness of American military policy in NATO. By reducing the role of conventional arms in favor of nuclear weapons and by putting the emphasis on retaliation, weapons for a war none wanted had been forged. For lack of "intermediate" means, the United States and NATO were led to an impossible choice between total war and total abandonment of a position; in its political and moral consequences, the latter could appear to be capitulation to an enemy more skilled in tactics and more capable of applying pressure. In November, 1956, the Western powers drew back from the threat of general war, both in abandoning the Suez operation and in refusing to give the legitimate Hungarian Government the protection it asked against foreign intervention. And the Soviet Union did not hesitate to brandish the threat of her guided missiles against the English and French at the same time as she put down the revolution in Budapest.

Thus, the West, at the end of 1956, found itself weakened and even more divided. Several months passed before it could absorb all the economic and political repercussions of the crisis. The difficulties in supplying oil—which only pointed up Europe's dependence on the Middle East and her American ally—were aggravated by their effect on the financial equilibrium and the balance of payments. In England, the prestige of the Conservative Government was so greatly shaken that for a while it seemed doubtful whether it could stay in power; all the firmness and cleverness that Macmillan hid behind his apparent nonchalance would be needed to save the day. In France, where a minority government had been in power for some time, the political effects of Suez were less immediately threatening, despite the general consternation. Indeed, many Frenchmen had seen the Suez campaign as a means of ending Egypt's intervention in Algeria and regretted its premature end. But Mollet's position was nonetheless shaken. To the socialist left wing and the partisans of a liberal colonial policy, he was a reactionary nationalist and a traitor to the cause of socialism, although this did not gain him the support of the right. The humiliation of the Suez failure was most deeply felt in the army, and its resentments aggravated the *malaise* of a nation that felt itself without a government.

In these dramatic circumstances—with the Atlantic Alliance threatened with collapse and the West suddenly aware of its weakness and isolation—Europeans, like Americans, sought some comfort in the thought that the Soviet world was also going through a time of troubles. The victories the Soviet leaders could chalk up to their credit were diminished by the conditions in which they had been won, by the revelation to the entire world of the tensions in the Soviet empire. Official explanations of scheming reactionary circles fooled no one. What had taken place in Budapest was not a small riot but a real revolution against a government whose only support came from outside the country and a brutal repression by a foreign army. Actually, the shock produced by this event in the West undoubtedly contributed to limiting the political repercussions of the Suez expedition. For it spread confusion among the left-wing circles that were inclined to believe in the possibility of peaceful coexistence and even among the Communist parties, now too busy re-establishing discipline and doctrinal unity to exploit the crisis created by the bumbling of the French and British governments. The Hungarian Revolution also tightened the Western bonds that internal tensions had threatened to break; the perspectives it half opened up and the threats to which it had given rise reminded everyone of the fragility and uncertainty of Europe's eastern frontier.

{ 7 }

Europe's Resurgence

The dramatic history of the efforts made by Western nations to save their common heritage—threatened by revolutionary forces that were destroying age-old economic, social, and political structures—admirably demonstrates the maxim that nothing great is done without despairing. Faced with the prospect of a break-up in the Atlantic Alliance, which would condemn a community on which men sought to confer a common political conscience and which, by the same token, would kill all hope for the integration of Europe, Europe now responded with a new outburst of energy.

And from this grew the drive toward what is called the European "resurgence" (*relance*). There had been, without doubt, some discouraging moments. The resignation of Jean Monnet in November, 1954, from his post as President of the High Authority of the Coal and Steel Community symbolized the "Europeans'" disappointment over the victory of nationalism. But this reaction was short-lived. During the following winter, European militants went back to work and, in the spring of 1955, were ready with new proposals.

The initiative this time came from the Benelux states. Ex-

perience had taught them prudence in dealing with the
French, Italian, and German governments. What they now
proposed was a fusion of national economies and a common
market realized through the progressive diminution of quantitative restrictions and customs duties. The harmonizing other
national regulations would also be done by stages, with a
simultaneous broadening of the common bases of economic
development in transport, energy, and the peaceful uses of
atomic energy. The authors of the plan had, in sum, tried
to avoid the expected complaints by proposing gradual integration. By combining several formulas and techniques of
integration, they satisfied simultaneously the "functionalists"
and "federalists." As they were careful not to insist on supranational powers for the common institutions they proposed,
their suggestions were favorably received by their Italian,
French, and German associates.

For this reason, the Messina Conference, which had started
with a certain skepticism, marked an important stage in the
history of Europe. Despite a few clashes, and perhaps because
of them, the ministers accepted the essential parts of the plan
submitted to them. The final communiqué, published on June
3, 1955, and cited often since, was not limited to setting the
goals: coordination of European policy in matters of transport,
energy production, and atomic energy; creation of a common
market; and harmonization of social policies. It also established
the procedures to be followed to reach these goals, and set a
deadline for the submission of a progress report by a committee of delegates.

Paul-Henri Spaak and his colleagues were quick to seize on
the once unhoped-for chance now offered them. Spaak, the
Belgian Minister of Foreign Affairs, to whom the presidency
of the intergovernmental committee was given, kept a group
of remarkably able experts working on a plan for more than
a year, concentrating first on the creation of a European
Atomic Energy Commission and then on the development of

a common market. Early in 1956, the members of the intergovernmental committee were ready to submit the general
outline of their project to the interested governments. But
they were not working alone. The Council of Europe was
following their studies attentively and gave them much encouragement. Moreover, Jean Monnet, now free of his official
duties, had once again entered into the fray. In October, 1955,
he had created the Action Committee for the United States of
Europe; its influence was felt from that time on at each stage
of the development of European integration. Coming at a time
when the "European movements" created immediately after
the war had lost their initial impetus or had been divided over
tactical and personal issues, the Committee took on the mission with which Spaak had once charged the Hague Congress:
"*bousculer les gouvernements.*"

The formula adopted by Jean Monnet was in fact very simple. It was a question of somehow surmounting the obstacles
created by national frontiers and the organization of parties
so as to join together in a common effort all men favorable to
the European idea. It was in this private organization that the
representatives of the principal political parties and labor
unions could, without publicity, develop a consensus. Members of the opposition would sit side by side with leaders of
the parties in power—Erich Ollenhauer and Herbert Wehner
with Kurt Kiesinger, Matteo Matteotti, Giovanni Malagodi,
and Amintore Fanfani, René Pleven, Robert Lecourt, and
Pierre Commin. It was not surprising, therefore, that the
declarations published from time to time by these men, each
of whom represented an important group of electors, contributed to orienting public opinion toward the idea of European union and to exerting a profound influence on the
governments.

All this became clear as early as January, 1956, when the
first resolution of the Committee was published. The Com-

mittee's members did not hesitate to speak in the name of the groups they represented:

> Our organizations, parties, and unions, meeting for the first time at a point beyond whatever may divide them on the national scene, are unanimous in their belief that the hopes of our people for better living conditions, justice, liberty, and peace will not be realized if national efforts are separated. Our countries must pool their resources and efforts. That is why we have taken the initiative in forming an Action Committee for the United States of Europe. The Committee will assure a unity of action among member organizations so as to establish, by successive, concrete stages, a United States of Europe.*

The tone was vigorous. The endorsement of the Messina Resolution, and, in particular, of the immediate creation of a European Atomic Energy Commission, was clear. Simple cooperation between governments was judged insufficient and found wanting. The states must delegate "the proper authority and the necessary common mandate to European institutions." The members of the Action Committee publicly promised to submit the declaration of principles that accompanied their manifesto for the approval of the legislatures of their respective countries and to urge their governments "to conclude without delay" a treaty in conformity with those principles.

This first resolution had a definite effect: Now the European rebirth was a matter of public knowledge. The public as well as the governments and legislatures to which the manifesto was addressed, were finally forced to consider the EURATOM whose creation was proposed in such imperative terms. And the idea was on the whole received well, mostly because it was not weighed down, as EDC had been, with a military burden. EURATOM was to be exclusively concerned with the peaceful uses of atomic energy, and a formula had

* *La Documentation Française, Articles et Documents,* No. 0.309 (January 21, 1956).

been found that made it possible to reconcile the necessity of control over nuclear power with a relative freedom of action for the users. Finally, while aid to the institutions of the Coal and Steel Community was taken into consideration, concentration of power that might have completely alienated the governments had been avoided.

The Action Committee for the United States of Europe naturally benefited from the work of the governmental delegates and their experts. But the service it rendered to the European cause in return was considerable. It is enough to observe the press during the first months of 1956 to note the progress of Europe's resurgence. The report of the intergovernmental committee that Spaak presented to the ministers of foreign affairs of the "Six," meeting in Venice on May 20, came at a favorable moment.

What was said in this oft-cited report was not new: Europe suffered anxiety over being caught between the United States, responsible for one-half of world production, and the Soviet Union, whose production was growing at the rate of 10 to 15 per cent per year. Encouraging as the progress of the last few years may have been, Europe could not continue its progress within its present economic framework:

> There is not a single automotive enterprise in Europe large enough to use economically and feasibly the most powerful American machines. Not one of the nations on this continent is capable of constructing large transport planes without outside aid. In the field of atomic energy, the knowledge acquired at great expense in several nations of Europe amounts to only a fraction of the knowledge the United States now puts freely at the disposal of its industries and of other countries. It would take years to produce a few thousand kilos of enriched uranium, of which America has just announced it can put a surplus of forty tons at the disposal of its industry and of other countries.*

* Comité intergouvernemental créé par la Conférence de Messine, *Rapport des chefs de délégations* (Brussels, 1956), p. 9.

This well-known theme, adroitly capitalizing on the myth of atomic revolution, introduced three proposals: (1) the establishment of a European Common Market among a limited group of states by means of a progressive fusion of separate markets, "the establishment of normal competitive conditions," and a harmonization of the development of the interested countries; (2) the formulation of "rules" and "procedures" for correcting the effects of state intervention or monopolies; and (3) the creation of new resources by opening up under-developed regions, reconverting outmoded plants, and allowing for the free circulation of means of production, men, and capital.

After this first detailed section, which Spaak evidently considered most imperative, the report presented EURATOM—that is, a European Atomic Energy Commission whose mission would be to develop research, to watch over the security of the population, to encourage investments, and to assure equal supplies of nuclear combustibles and the opening of outlets for atomic energy by the fusion of markets.

For both the Common Market and the atomic energy institutions, it was planned to create a council of ministers whose task would be to coordinate general policy and whose decisions would be made by unanimous vote; a European commission whose task would be the administration of common affairs; a court, perhaps an enlargement of the ECSC Court; and finally, an organization with parliamentary control, of which the Assembly of the Coal and Steel Community could form the base.

The third part of the report dealt with what was then called "sectors of urgent action"—supply of energy, air transport, postal and telecommunications—for which a certain degree of coordination was recommended.

The government reaction to the Spaak Report was positive. The threat of supranational organisms had been removed. "Let us organize as much as we can without resorting to the delegation of governmental powers." Such was the order Spaak gave to the members of his committee—or so it was claimed. The rule was observed and the beginning of negotiations thus facilitated. Spaak left Venice to continue the task of coordination he had assumed. (He had been appointed President of a Conference to be held in Brussels at the end of June to prepare a treaty setting up the Common Market and the Organization for Atomic Energy.)

The negotiations were, in fact, long and laborious. A great deal of resistance was encountered, especially over the establishment of a Common Market: It was necessary to take into account the relative weakness of France's balance of payments in comparison to Germany's strong position; it was necessary to overcome the distrust of French industrialists, many of whom shied away from the effort to adapt and modernize; it was necessary to take into consideration the particular conditions in southern Italy, to find applicable formulas for the agricultural sector and solutions that would be valid for the overseas territories.

With good will and some concessions to the most demanding or obstinate partners, agreement was finally reached. Other events during the summer and autumn of 1956, which showed up Europe's weakness in so cruel a light, contributed to the final *rapprochement*. The pressure of influential Europeans—in particular of the Action Committee for the United States of Europe, which had succeeded in obtaining favorable declarations from various national legislatures and which did not hesitate to propagandize—also played an important role. The two treaties setting up the European Economic Community and EURATOM were finally signed in Rome on March 25, 1957. After their ratification, Robert Schuman said in one of his speeches: "The confusion in the Atlantic world caused by the set-backs in Suez and in Hungary has stimulated the vote in favor of these European projects. Unexpectedly large majorities have approved the Rome Agreements."

The victory of the "Europeans," which the American Government enthusiastically welcomed as the first results of a policy it had encouraged and supported ever since 1945, was only partial, however. The Europe now being organized was only a small Europe. Great Britain had not been able to join it for fear of compromising the economic and political ties that bound her to the Commonwealth. Spain and Portugal, Greece and Turkey, Ireland and Iceland remained outside; so did Switzerland, Austria, and the Scandinavian countries. Why these refusals to join, when in fact the Treaty of Rome foresaw the possibility of widening the European Economic Community? The reasons invoked differed from country to country, but, beside the unique obstacles created by an underdeveloped region or difficulties in agricultural policy, the principal objection was that the common customs agreements established within the Common Market might reduce the trade enjoyed with countries that were not members of the EEC.

The nations invoking this argument were satisfied with a formula that was more flexible than the one proposed by the Six, for whom the creation of a Common Market was only a step toward the political integration of Europe. As members of the OEEC, they drew up a balance sheet of OEEC activities since 1949: about 85 per cent of inter-European exchange freed, with a resulting growth of 12 per cent in internal European commerce between 1948 and 1956 (compared with 54 per cent for the rest of the world); transferability of currencies among European countries, thanks to the institution of the European Payments Union; suppression of the major part of restrictions on services; the start of a full and systematic examination "of the economic, financial, budgetary, and investment policies of its members"; creation of a minis-

terial committee on food and agriculture; beginning of the
free movement of manpower; creation of a European Pro-
✓ ductivity Agency and a European Nuclear Energy Agency;
and, following the Suez crisis, control over the division of the
oil supply of Europe.

In view of the evident progress made by a method of collaboration that took account of diverse national conditions, it
was difficult, outside the group of the Six, to see the need for
hastening the development by confining oneself to the more
rigid structures of the Common Market. At the same time,
however, the "outer" nations feared the consequences of the
discrimination that would result from the progressive lowering of tariff barriers among the members of the EEC. A
compromise formula was sought—the creation of a free trade
zone whose members, while progressively eliminating quantitative restrictions and tariffs, would control their own com-
mercial policies toward states outside the zone.

This solution, first suggested in July, 1956, was most ingenious. Clearly circumscribed, marked by certain precaution-
ary measures aimed, in particular, at defining the origin of
products, it could help avoid the break-up of Europe that the
initiative of the Six risked bringing about. It was favorably
looked on by "Europeans" such as Jean Monnet, who campaigned vigorously for its creation, and also by several of the
signatories of the Treaty of Rome, who feared the consequences of an economic war and were favorable to an agreement. In the Council of Europe, the current of opinion in
favor of economic cooperation between the Six and the other
European countries was gaining strength.

Certain states, however, France above all, were intransigent from the very beginning. The technical difficulty of
defining the origin of products imported from the free trade
zone to the Common Market countries was pointed to; there
was anger over the attempt to enjoy the advantages of the
Common Market without assuming its burdens—the harmoni-

zation of economic policies and social-welfare charges, which allowed the establishment of a system of normal competition. That was a point on which French management was particularly clear. "To do a sound job," we read in a note published late in 1956 by the National Confederation of French Employers and intended for the French negotiators, "we must put the accent less on the time limits for the reduction of customs duties and more on the bond that *must* exist between these reductions and the other elements in the Common Market (harmonization of economic, social, and fiscal legislation and policies, progressive liberation of the circulation of manpower and capital)."*

Truth to tell, it was possible that in spite of this intransigence, born of a long protectionist tradition, some means of accommodation would be found. The difficulties were not, however, exclusively economic or technical, but also political. The debate focused on the very concept of European collaboration. It set against each other the partisans of "United Europe"—that is, of a politically and economically integrated Europe whose component states would progressively abdicate their sovereignty for the benefit of a truly European government—and the partisans of "European cooperation," who, valuing the strength and importance of national differences, strove to reconcile unity and diversity, affirming that it was in liberalizing trade practices and lowering tariffs that the basic conditions of true European collaboration could be created.

These debates over method were still further complicated by the old Franco-British rivalry. Since the early years of the twentieth century, these two nations had always joined together when faced with common dangers, but their styles of life and thought differed too greatly for them ever to agree naturally on policies, which were, moreover, strongly influ-

* Conseil national du Patronat francais, *Le projet de marché commun européen*, supplement to the Bulletin No. 153 of the Conseil (Paris, 1956), pp. 12–13.

enced by the difference in their geographical situations. The French would have liked to weld Great Britain more closely to Europe. They had insisted on it at the time of the Schuman Plan and also when the European Defense Community was being debated. Fearing then a confrontation with Germany, they needed the British presence to help them maintain balance. But the refusal of the British government at that point had created a resentment that was frequently expressed during the debates over ratification. Now that cordial relations and a climate of reciprocal confidence had been established with the Federal Republic, the desire to attract England, whose presence might disturb this promising collaboration, was less strong; a certain definite reserve was noticeable, mixed with some bitterness and desire for revenge. Europe was in the process of organizing herself; if she was disposed to widen her circle and admit her British neighbor, she would not tolerate the new arrival, as a condition of her participation, imposing her own concept of integration. Henceforth, it was up to Great Britain to make the necessary effort to adapt.

Such was the way that many Frenchmen reasoned, particularly those who assumed the responsibility for France's European policy. It was therefore not surprising that negotiations went slowly. Since the beginning of 1957, the Council of the OEEC had been convinced that a free trade zone including the Common Market was technically possible, and it had decided to negotiate with the member states of the European Economic Community on that basis.* But it was necessary to wait for the end of the ratification debates, and it was not until the autumn of 1957 that consideration of the problem was begun—cautiously, even then.

As for NATO, it had been striving to rectify its most apparent shortcomings. Some months before the Suez crisis, the

* *Report on the possibility of creating a free trade area* (OEEC: Paris, January, 1957).

North Atlantic Council had decided to create a Committee on
Nonmilitary Cooperation, with the job of presenting recommendations to the Council on measures to further cooperation in nonmilitary fields among NATO members and to
increase unity in the Atlantic Community. The task of this
three-man committee (called the "Three Wise Men" in the
nonsensical style of the time) was not an easy one, as later
events, brutally emphasizing the need for a re-examination of
the policy of NATO's member states, amply demonstrated.
The members of the North Atlantic Council, meeting in
December, 1956, were only too aware of this and hastened to
ratify the recommendations submitted to them.

What, then, did the Three Wise Men say? "It has become
increasingly realized since the Treaty was signed that security
is today far more than a military matter. The strengthening
of political consultation and economic cooperation, the public
understanding, all these can be as important, or even more
important, for the protection of the security of a nation, or
an alliance, as the building of a battleship or the equipping
of an army."*

This was a truism, as was the statement that the Soviet
Union was seeking to win over countries "by economic means
and by political subversion." George Kennan, in an article published in July, 1947, in *Foreign Affairs*, had already defined
Soviet conduct in analogous terms and proposed a containment policy that aimed precisely at the political and economic struggle. But for the Three Wise Men, it seemed to
be a new problem posing an "additional challenge" to NATO.
The North Atlantic Alliance had been created to meet a military challenge; it had been marked from the outset by the
difficulties caused by the Berlin Blockade and the Korean
War; and it had progressively lost sight of the global nature
of the Soviet offensive. Khrushchev had now taken it upon

* "Non-Military Cooperation in NATO," *NATO Letter*, Vol. V, Special
Supplement No. 1, section 15 (January, 1957).

himself to remind his Atlantic opponents of what the permanent objectives of Soviet foreign policy were, and to draw
their attention to the variety of means at his command. Thus
the obligation followed to proceed to a readaptation. The
report of the Three Wise Men insisted on the need to develop
an "Atlantic Community," which it defined as "the permanent
association of the free Atlantic peoples for the promotion of
their greater unity and the protection and the advancement of
the interests which, as free democracies, they have in common."* This association, they said, was the result of a historical evolution dominated by the coming of the nuclear age, in
which a state can no longer progress or even survive by its
own means alone. The maintenance and development of the
Atlantic Community, whose existence would not be incompatible with that of a United Europe, implied a tightening up
of international collaboration at all levels and in all fields—
whether on questions of national policies or in economic, scientific, and cultural exchanges.

The approval given to the Three Wise Men's report should
have encouraged a new beginning. It had been acknowledged
that the interests of NATO members "are not confined to the
area covered by the Treaty" and that, consequently, a coordination of national foreign policies in the planning stage
was indispensable. That exchanges of information were necessary to scientific development had already been admitted, and
the development of cooperation in cultural affairs had already
been considered.

But it did not follow that concrete effects would come of
these acknowledgments. The basic problems had not been
resolved. The Government of the United States was no more
willing than it had been before to give moral support to the
policies of its French and British allies in Africa. It showed
scarcely any enthusiasm for a scientific collaboration that

* *Ibid.*, section 28.

would lead to an enlargement of the nuclear club. If it suited its convenience (so long as it did not have intercontinental missiles) to build launching pads on the territory of its European allies, it nevertheless did not wish to lose control over the use of atomic missiles. The dangers of divided responsibilities seemed too serious. This was an attitude that some of the allies had difficulty in understanding. France was particularly sensitive, since Anglo-American collaboration in the atomic field relegated her to a lower level of power.

Thus, it was not surprising that the launching of the first Sputnik in the autumn of 1957 provoked a general and intense anxiety. Americans, who had long been convinced of their technical superiority, were stunned by the news that their Soviet rivals had surpassed them in the "race in space." The Administration was forced by the pressure of public opinion to abandon its studied calm and to take steps to reorganize its "research and development" projects, steps that its critics had demanded for a long time. In Europe, opinion was divided between admiration, fear, and *Schadenfreude*. Europeans were aware simultaneously of the potentials of the great Russian people and the power of their authoritarian regime. At the same time, the fear developed that the Soviet Union might use this doubtless momentary advantage. And one could not help feeling some irony in regard to the United States—once so self-assured that she would not deign to allow her allies to join in her researches. Perhaps now she might re-examine the conditions of Atlantic collaboration and share her secrets more generously.

To this new Soviet challenge—a peaceful challenge, true, but one that Moscow hastened to exploit, by increasing its involvement with nations who wished to develop atomic power or who were amenable to the installation of launching pads on their soil—NATO responded with a demonstration of its unity that was clearly more spectacular than effective. The heads of the allied governments, with the President of the United States in the lead, met in Paris for a session of the North Atlantic Council. After the usual introductory survey of the situation, several decisions were made: to establish launching pads for atomic missiles in Europe that would be regulated by direct agreement between the Supreme Allied Commander of Europe and the state concerned; to set up a scientific commission, including experts from each member state, to study the means of strengthening scientific cooperation.

Some months later, a communiqué issued at the end of a North Atlantic Council meeting announced new progress in the establishment of a "true community of free nations. Within this community, to a degree unprecedented in history, countries are carrying out a policy of close co-operation in peacetime without abandoning their independence. Every effort [the communiqué added] should be made to ensure economic prosperity, notably by the expansion of international trade and by aid to underdeveloped countries."* Spaak added: "It is not only a question of simple assurances or of simple hopes."

It is true that everyone had the best intentions; it is certain that within NATO itself an effort had been made to translate into action the evidently unanimous desire for close collaboration. Other encouragement came, moreover, from outside. An attempt was made to marshall public opinion in favor of the establishment of an Atlantic Community. Conferences followed one after the other, bringing together intellectuals and politicians from Europe and America, animated by the hope of giving roots to a military alliance born of a common past. There is, it was loudly affirmed, an Atlantic Civilization. So it was said at Bruges during the Atlantic Conference of September, 1957, and it was repeated at the NATO Parliamentarians' Conference in November.

* Final communiqué of the NATO Council ministerial meeting, Copenhagen, May 7, 1958, in *Documents on International Affairs*, pp. 356–57.

But the coordination of national policies was no easier than it had been before. If the members of the Atlantic Community approved Anglo-American intervention in Lebanon, the tension caused by the sudden recrudescence of Chinese activity before Formosa revealed the United States to be in isolation. And the United States abstention in the U.N. vote on Algeria reminded the French Government that its allies intended to keep their distance.

Preoccupying as the crises were that dotted the year 1958 —contributing to a kind of a quasi-permanent tension—serious as the Iraq revolution first seemed in the West, it was in France that the most dramatic event took place, and the one with the direst consequences for Europe and the West: the fall of the Fourth Republic.

It had been expected. For years, the decline of governmental authority resulting from the impossibility of forming a majority in favor of one political policy had been apparent to all. This refusal to make the necessary choices was an aspect of the intellectualism that dominated French politics, of the tendency to reduce politics to a battle of ideas that did not necessarily correspond to reality—over principles that neither side consistently respected, over the inability to cleanse a historical heritage and isolate from it the problems of the present and future, and over the fear of taking the risks which that choice implied. The Revolution had become a cult. It was no longer an instrument of combat.

Yet to this failing in their state, the French seemed easily to accommodate themselves. They had become accustomed to organizing their lives outside that of their government. A central administration sufficed, they thought, to assure a continuity in the principal services of which the nation had need.

But this was not true in the conduct of foreign policy. There it was not possible to evade the choices imposed by the evolution of foreign affairs in which France was involved.

Because it did not measure the international consequences of the weakening of state authority, the Third Republic had fallen. The Fourth Republic met the same fate, and for the same reasons.

The necessity of choice was imposed by Algeria. For almost four years, the French had been involved in an armed struggle that had grown almost daily until it absorbed more than 400,000 men. It was not that the enemy's forces were large—several thousand or tens of thousands of men at the most—but that they were difficult to meet in battle. The countryside was vast, inaccessible in some places, a favorable terrain for the guerrilla tactics practiced by the FLN, who depended on a Muslim population that they either terrorized or had won over, and who benefited from the support of neighboring Arab countries. In France, the war was not popular. It kept men who could be useful elsewhere out of the country. It used up vital resources and consequently impeded the economic expansion of the country. Above all, it seemed contrary to the principle of self-determination, of which the French were proud to claim a remote authorship and to which the whole world adhered. To continue the war until the revolutionary forces were destroyed was to hold fast to an outmoded colonialism in an enterprise that was bound to be a dead end.

But giving in would mean risking the loss not only of Algeria but of access to Africa and particularly to the Sahara, which was only just beginning to be exploited and whose resources offered France the chance to liberate herself, in part at least, from the political liabilities incurred by her need for a steady flow of oil. And in any case, could one give in? The relation of Algeria to France was different from that of Morocco or Tunisia. It was a question of a territory with a powerful minority of Frenchmen who considered Algeria their home and who could not conceive of being forced to leave. These Algerian Frenchmen were resolved to fight on.

Threatened in their daily existence and by their future, they watched with growing anger the debates in France between the advocates and opponents of negotiation with the leaders of the Revolution, and the hesitations of the government. And they were not alone: Impatience grew in the army as well. It grew as the war dragged on, as it took on new forms that demanded new matériel and combat methods, as the army ran up against the unremitting opposition of a hostile and indifferent population (although they were fighting on territory they considered French), as they were never able to count on the support of either policy-makers or public opinion. The officer corps—many of whose members had fought in Indochina, whence they had returned discouraged and humiliated—felt that French indecision was leading to a new capitulation they did not want. Armed with the Indochinese experience, they thought they were strong enough to defeat the revolt provided they were given the means. They were ready to support the French who would refuse to capitulate. Thus the army found itself allied with the French Algerians and a popular movement brought them together to the steps of the government palace on May 13, 1958. The army was there because its leaders had brought it there, but also because it could not do otherwise. Still, it was a delicate situation, and the army's attitude—or at least that of its commander in chief, General Salan—remained ambiguous.

In France, where the public had been prepared for riots but not for this brutal challenge to the authority of the government, there was general confusion. The ministers hesitated, and the divided National Assembly could give them neither advice nor support. The Government, unable to count on the police or the army, was without means of action, and the Assembly lacked the confidence of the people.

For several days, the country stood poised on the threshold of civil war. But nothing happened except speeches, proclamations, and demonstrations. The evocation of a great heri-

tage found no more response than did the appeal to form an
underground movement as during World War II. The
French, in fact, did not want a revolution. Was this because
of lassitude? Or was it rather due to the conservatism of the
rural and middle classes, their numbers swelled with the
improvements in living conditions of the modern age?

In these circumstances, the return of General de Gaulle
to the political scene was greeted with a sigh of relief. Despite
his postwar failures, he had retained his moral authority. He
was still a national hero and, for all those who had fought with
him, he was still a leader. He was respected both for his integrity and for his intellectual qualities. (Charles de Gaulle
was a writer, and that was something which counted in
France.) The political reorganization, prepared in laborious
negotiation, was, moreover, facilitated by his measured tone
and flexible tactics, for which people were all the more grateful as they had not expected it.

A period of intensive work began. The Assembly had col-
lapsed, and the new government had a free hand to carry out
the reforms it had announced. In Algeria, the army was slowly
taken in hand and the men of May 13 "put in place." The
Constitution of the Fifth Republic, proposed after only a few
months, was accepted by a large majority on September 28.
A whole series of problems that previous governments had
tackled but been unable to resolve were now dealt with.
French administration was still operating according to a
structure established by Bonaparte. A process of modernization began immediately. Naturally, these reforms, carried
through in double time in an almost consular style, did not
fail to arouse criticism. But resistance was relatively weak and
focused more on particular points of application than on the
whole, for intelligent men realized the need for this long-
deferred modernization of the administrative apparatus. Some
even went so far as to say that bolder steps could be taken.

As for the Constitution, it was exactly what was to be

expected, given the ideas of the head of the government: It gave to the President of the Republic all the powers needed to allow him to guide the policy of the nation; the prime minister was relegated to a secondary position. As for the Assembly and Senate, which kept their essential prerogatives, of which voting on the budget was not the least important, all possibility of returning to a parliamentary government was excluded, insofar as the President of the Republic determined to use the power of dissolution the Constitution gave him—a presidential republic, in other words, made to order for the man to whom everything pointed as the first President.

This Fifth Republic was at the same time the center of a federation of states. The Constitution had provided for the creation of a Community; the President of the Republic would also be its President. It offered Madagascar and the other member states of the French Union the option of total independence or membership in the Community. Guinea chose independence, and all the others voted for collaboration with France within the Community.

Thus, from the very beginning, the Fifth Republic was shot through with apparently contradictory strains. The reaction against the excesses of parliamentarianism had led to a strengthening of executive powers and to the victory of a democracy that some called Bonapartist. But simultaneously, the new regime offered to the peoples dependent on France a plan for association the Fourth Republic had not dared to propose. This port of liberalism was a luxury that only a state sure of its authority could allow itself.

It was not surprising that criticism rained down on the Fifth Republic from all quarters. On the extreme right and left, opponents rose up against a regime considered far too weak to contain the strength and purpose now proposed. Men of the Fourth Republic were inclined to be skeptical, even hostile, especially after the elections that voted in a "die-hard" Assembly. France, in sum, put its trust more in the man than in his associates or in the institutions he set up. But everyone knew that one day France would be without De Gaulle. And that knowledge gave rise to a vague feeling that the nation was embarking on an adventure that one could only hope would be transformed into a positive experience—provided that an end could be put to the war in Algeria.

Europe also watched and waited. Like the United States, she had followed the ups and downs of the French crisis, divided between fear and hope. Like the French, indeed like the whole world, Europe knew that the day would come when France would have to confront certain fundamental questions, and she also knew that all the plans of past years, all the efforts for the recovery of the West and of the Atlantic world, depended on the outcome of this crisis. The Coal and Steel Community, the Common Market, EURATOM, the Atlantic Pact—all these might be threatened by a revolution that, at one blow, could alter the power balance between the Soviet Union and the Western powers. Consequently, the arrival of General de Gaulle produced the same reaction in Europe as it did in France. Whatever the fears inspired by De Gaulle's touchy patriotism and demands for France, there was a feeling of reassurance. And this feeling intensified as the conviction grew that France would be faithful to her alliances and would honor her obligations. Moreover, the re-establishment of governmental authority of the state, evidenced at the diplomatic level by a return to classic methods and by a rigorous preservation of secrecy, quickly had its effects. France once again had the international audience she had lost.

But in Europe, deadlines were approaching. The first reduction of tariffs planned for the Common Market was to take place on January 1, 1959. The French crisis had delayed negotiations concerning the free trade zone, which had been hindered by French intransigence. Proponents of a free trade zone persisted in the hope that a compromise solution was possible. But General de Gaulle and his principal collaborators had not, in previous years, shown much enthusiasm for far-reaching integration. They preferred the Europe of independent states to the United Europe of Robert Schuman. Yet the hope was that they would be more flexible than their predecessors. This was not to be the case. On the contrary, the French Government showed that it considered itself bound by the Treaty of Rome and emphatically demonstrated that it valued a close Franco-German collaboration and that it had reservations about the United Kingdom. The maneuver was so clear, the intention so obvious that one wondered for a moment whether General de Gaulle (who in his *Mémoires* had written of his growing impatience with Anglo-Saxon tutelage during the war) had not seized the opportunity to take revenge. But the real explanation was simpler and more likely: What De Gaulle wanted was to base his policy on a Europe whose unification was in the interest of France, in order that he could better make his influence felt in the tripartite directory he wished to see established in NATO. It was for this same reason that he decided to construct a French atomic bomb and to force his way into the nuclear club— from which the English even more than the Americans would have liked to bar France.

The new French policy of greater independence from the United States (toward which, it was felt, preceding governments had not shown the required reserve) implied a close collaboration among the European allies and a common acceptance of plans worked out within the Europe of the Six. By agreeing to the free trade zone, one ran the risk of compromising the political objectives of integration. Moreover, strong pressures were exercised in favor of a refusal. The Confederation of French Employers, which, after some hesitation, had opted for the Common Market, did not even wish to talk of a free trade zone. Now, the elections were close at hand. And the first duty of the government was to end this delicate transition period and assure a solid electoral basis for the new Fifth Republic. Could it, given the state of the French economy and finances, afford the luxury of widening the circle of its competitors without first making the necessary reforms? Charles de Gaulle is, after all, a pragmatist. After considering the difficulties posed by a compromise, he allowed the crisis to break that members of the OEEC had hoped to avert. And simultaneously, he softened its political and economic effects by adopting a plan drawn up by Jacques Rueff and proposed by Antoine Pinay.

In fact, cutting the existing import tariff by 90 per cent for goods from member countries of the OEEC and by 50 per cent for imports from the dollar zone (decided on late in December, 1958), the devaluation of the franc by 15 per cent, accompanied by the re-establishment of convertibility for nonresidents, made a favorable impression abroad and particularly in those OEEC countries where the rather brutal break-off in negotiations had been especially disturbing—all the more because these decisions were matched by a number of measures aimed to produce a real overhauling of the French economy, so as to render it competitive once again.

As the British Government had made a parallel decision to re-establish the convertibility of the pound for nonresidents, the meeting of the Council of Ministers of the OEEC of January, 1959, convened in a somewhat less tense atmosphere than that which had prevailed in December. There was, indeed, full awareness that the measures the two governments had taken and the political intentions they revealed ought—insofar as they produced the desired effects and the economic situation improved—to permit a new and more favorable examination of the conditions for European economic cooperation. For the establishment of the Common Market had not destroyed the hopes nourished in most European countries for new negotiations. In the Federal Republic, the then Minister of Economic Affairs, Ludwig Erhard, made no secret of his intention to avoid a division in Europe at any cost, for the consequences of it for the German economy would be unfortunate. The governments of the Benelux countries and Italy likewise did not hide their desire to renew contacts with one another. And the same feelings were shared by the "Non-Six," who, encouraged by the fear of economic discrimination, took new initiatives. No one was surprised to learn, in the spring of 1959, that Great Britain, the Scandinavian countries, Switzerland, Austria, and Portugal were in the process of studying the creation of a "small free trade zone," which its promoters regarded as a regroupment of forces essential to renewed negotiations under conditions more advantageous than those of 1958.

{ 8 }

Economic Progress and Political Complications: 1959-60

The last decade has been a very dynamic period for the economy of Western Europe. Production potential has enormously expanded; consumption has been raised to levels which warrant being called a new standard of living; and new methods of cooperation have been evolved which have shown their worth.*

Such was the judgment on Western Europe's economic evolution between 1947 and 1957 contained in an OEEC report published in April, 1958.

The authors of the report, assessing the work in which they themselves had participated, expressed understandable satisfaction. And they could cite eloquent facts and figures to support their conclusions.

In 1947, "the number of dwellings in the Western European countries involved in the war was 7 per cent below the prewar level,"† while the population had grown by 8 per

* *A Decade of Cooperation: Achievements and Perspectives* (OEEC: Paris, 1958), p. 139.
† *Ibid.*, p. 24.

cent. The slowness of the coal and steel industry's recovery was creating bottlenecks. Exports reached only 70 per cent of prewar volume; despite the need, imports stood at only 90 per cent of the prewar figure. Net receipts from foreign investments, transportation, and other sources, which in 1938 had covered almost the entire trade deficit, were now insignificant. The year 1947 had been marked by a large deficit in the balance of current payments and, despite external aid amounting to nearly $6 billion, West European gold and dollar reserves had been "punctured" in the amount of about $2.5 billion. The number of freight cars in use and the tonnage of the merchant fleet were also less than before the war. The number of housing units needed was estimated at 7 million.

In 1957, the situation in Western Europe, or more exactly in the member states of the Organization for European Economic Cooperation, was quite different. The market price of the gross national product was $234 billion, as against $148 billion in 1938. Grain production rose from 47 million metric tons in 1947 to 86 million in 1957; electric power, from 179 billion kilowatt hours to 409 billion; steel, from 31 million metric tons to 88 million; petroleum products, from 11 to 100 million metric tons. During the same period, per-capita consumption rose from $380 to $530, while meat consumption rose from 31 to 47 kilos. There were 52 automobiles per 1,000 persons, as against 15 in 1947, and construction of housing units was progressing at the rate of 7 per 1,000 persons, as against 2 per 1,000 in 1947.

These are, of course, Continental figures or averages that do not reveal the differences in living conditions, or rather, in development, between one country and another, particularly the situation in the underdeveloped regions of southern Europe. *The Economic Survey of Europe in 1958,* published by by the U. N. Economic Commission for Europe, remarked that the "expansion was faster in the industrialized countries

of north and northwestern Europe than in the less developed
countries of the south and in Ireland; per-capita gross national
product rose by over two-fifths in the former group and by
approximately one-quarter in the latter.* A country-by-coun-
try examination shows these contrasts still more clearly: While
in Germany and Austria the per capita GNP surpassed the prewar level by two-thirds, and in Belgium, France, Switzerland,
Sweden, and Norway by 40 per cent, the growth had only
been 25 per cent in the United Kingdom and Denmark, and
7 per cent in Greece. A study of per-capita private consumption showing that the spread in levels of consumption between the industrialized and less developed regions of Europe
had widened only confirms these observations.

But it was nonetheless true that the picture was a positive
one on the whole. As serious as the economic problems in
some of the less developed countries or regions, as real as the
difficulties (especially the political ones) confronting governments that tried to reconcile expansion of production with a
high employment level, financial stability, and a balance of
payments, the picture of Western Europe at the beginning
of 1959 was considerably more encouraging than that of the
immediate postwar period.

From all sides—not only from Germany, but from Italy,
France, and even Great Britain—came positive and optimistic
reports. The most enthusiastic partisans of European unity did
not dispute that this economic recovery created favorable
conditions for the European Economic Community. They
could deny neither the real merits of the OEEC and the
European Payments Union nor the beneficial effect of these
organizations on the economic life of the member countries.

It was thus in a favorable climate that the new attempt at
European integration began, to be borne forward by an
economy in full expansion. The widespread feeling that the

* Geneva, 1958. Chapter 5, p. 2.

decisive step had now been taken, that the Common Market was an irrevocable fact, encouraged everyone to make plans to use the new situation to the best possible advantage. Leaders in private industry who, particularly in France, had been rather slow to rally to the cause of Europe advocated by political groups, proceeded immediately with structural transformations which, in their view, the requirements and potentials of a great economic market made imperative. For it was essential, in order to survive the competition, to establish favorable take-off positions as quickly as possible. Starting early in 1959, and following one upon another, merger agreements among industries, various sorts of *ententes* aimed at creating a division of labor and coordination of production, meetings among professional groups (sometimes resulting in larger groups embracing all six countries), financial arrangements—all these were arranged, encouraged, and codified.

The political decision to form the Common Market thus led to a complete transformation of the economic infrastructure of the Europe of the Six. Action was taken not on the basis of the existing situation, but of a projection of what Europe would be like in 1970. And that projection—it was still nothing more than a myth—became reality even sooner than its creators expected. The interaction of myth and reality, which is perhaps not very surprising to a historian, was nonetheless a surprise to the men of the Common Market from the moment its effects were noted.

The fever that took hold in business circles soon spread beyond the Europe of the Six; enterprises in other European countries or in the United States did not want to be left behind, and they quickly sought to position themselves within the Market before it was too late. The steps taken by them contributed to the success of the very community from which they feared exclusion and, by the same token, strengthened not only its economic, but also its symbolic value. For the Six, who in the initial phase had had to overcome so many obstacles to their plans for common institutions, this was powerful encouragement; through the confidence it created, often contradictory interests were reconciled.

The third general report of the European Economic Commission sounded, therefore, like a victory bulletin:

> The year 1959 has been marked by spectacular developments, which bear witness to the interest of economic groups in the Common Market and to their confidence in its future. Above all, there has been great expansion in intra-Community commercial trade, the value of which, in relation to the corresponding period of the previous year, rose by 16 per cent in the second quarter, 22 per cent in the third quarter, and 26 per cent in the fourth quarter. It is interesting to note that this growth of intra-Community trade has not occurred at the expense of trade with other countries, the value of which, for all of 1959, grew by 8 per cent in relation to 1958, a considerable increase in any case.
>
> But how is this difference in levels of growth to be explained? It cannot be attributed uniquely to the economic expansion of the member countries or to the special conditions created within the Community: The lowering of customs duties of January 1, 1959, has been widely extended to outside countries, as have been many other liberalizing measures. What should be noted is that the economic sectors, anticipating, as it were, the implementation of the Treaty, are "playing the Community" and are tending more and more to place their development programs and trade patterns in the context of a functioning Common Market. No doubt, it is necessary to qualify this general picture to take account of special reactions from this group or that country, but the tendency is there nonetheless.*

Statistics on EEC trade during 1960 were just as optimistic. Intra-Community trade continued to progress; in the first half of 1960 its total value increased by more than 12 per cent over the second half of 1959. Although the growth of trade with other outside countries was smaller, it was nonetheless considerable.

* *La Documentation française: Notes et études documentaires*, No. 2729, December 14, 1960.

But these were successes of a Europe that, despite every-thing, was still divided. It was divided economically by the Common Market's customs barrier, whose importance, insignificant at the beginning, was to increase with the progressive lowering of intra-Community tariffs. It was divided politically by the well-known objective for which the promoters of the EEC aimed—the creation of a European state—the EEC being only a means, a stage through which it was necessary to pass in order to take account of nationalistic resistance. The third EEC report discussed this accelerated lowering of tariffs: "The European Commission wishes to make clear the political importance it attaches to this acceleration, beyond the economic benefits expected from it for both the Community itself and its partners in the Western world. The internal strengthening it offers . . . must confirm, by bypassing national differences, the movement toward union to which the six states have become committed by signing the Rome Treaty."

Those states that for varying reasons had been unable to accept the integration formula adopted by the Six had been put into a difficult position through the breakdown of negotiations for the establishment of a free trade zone. Their reply —the only possible one from the moment they excluded joining the Six or concluding bilateral economic agreements—was to be the creation of a "small free trade zone." The United Kingdom, Norway, Denmark, Sweden, Switzerland, Austria, and Portugal began negotiations to this end in February, 1959. Due to the fact that the basic problems and technical questions had already been worked through in the discussions of 1957–58, the negotiations proceeded quickly, and in July, 1959, a basic agreement was reached on the creation of the European Free Trade Association. On November 20, after a ministerial session held in Stockholm, the convention was signed.

The European Free Trade Association did not aim for

political union of European states. It did not seek a confederation of states set up in opposition to the European Federation toward which the Common Market was tending. A group of nations that, by virtue of their historic traditions, incarnated the variety of European affairs, it wished to keep any limitations on national sovereignty to a minimum and aimed only for a flexible coordination of economic policies: A pamphlet put out to explain the European Free Trade Association (bearing the significant title "The Stockholm Convention and Freer World Trade") expressed it thus: "Like any free trade area, the EFTA will confer upon member countries all the advantages of an enlarged home market, further developments in the division of labour, and a more efficient allocation of resources. Increasing activity is likely to add, moreover, to the demand for imports from all sources, and the outward-looking character of the arrangements will allow outside countries also to share in the benefits."* The principal provision of the Convention, therefore, foresaw the gradual elimination of tariffs over the next ten-year period, the first 20 per cent reduction coming on July 1, 1960, and the others spread over the entire period so as to harmonize with the pattern set by the EEC. To this basic clause were added special measures imposed by the need to reconcile the requirements of a free trade zone with the freedom reserved by member states as concerns their economic policy regarding nonmember states.

This desire to focus the efforts on developing economic exchanges and to limit collaboration to this field was expressed in the actual organization of the EEC. In order to avoid a system in which Common institutions would become dominant, provision was made not only for a Council where all member states would have one vote, but also for a consultative committee composed of representatives of groups par-

* EFTA: Stockholm, 1959, p. 21.

ticipating in the economic life of the member states. As for the Secretariat—an essential factor—it was made clear from the beginning that its size and power would be limited. There was no question of creating an administrative apparatus preparative for a European government, like the European Commission at Brussels.

Thus, once again, the differences in approach to intra-European collaboration were underscored: On the one hand, there were the partisans of economic integration who carried it to its extreme political consequences; on the other, there were those who wanted ever-increasing economic cooperation, but of a sort that would respect European differences and consequently the sovereignty of individual states. A new battle was beginning, and it would be a bitter one. To the members of the EFTA, who complained that they were the objects of discrimination and protested against the desire in some quarters to monopolize the idea of "Europe" for the benefit of a single centralizing concept, spokesmen for the Common Market replied that their club was not exclusive, that it was open to all who would fulfill the conditions for membership, and that, since unity of forces was indispensable to the security of Europe, those who refused to make this effort were betraying the European cause.

Grave as the conflict was, however, an awareness of common interests did nonetheless continue to exist. It had been constantly strengthened during the fifteen years since the end of the war, and had passed out of the salons and cafés into the parliaments, offices, and universities. Indeed, it had penetrated into the deepest layers of public opinion. Even those who insisted on the diversity of geographic conditions and historical traditions now loudly proclaimed themselves "Europeans." The members of the EFTA did not lose the opportunity to point out that they had joined together only in order to be in a better position to convince their vis-à-vis in the Common Market of the necessity of collaboration. And they were not alone in their wish to renew negotiations. Within the Six, the Benelux states (the Netherlands in particular) openly expressed their wish to see "little Europe" enlarged. In the German Federal Republic, where officials were more sensitive to the possible economic repercussions of the EFTA's creation, the current of opinion favorable to a resumption of discussions was stronger. Dr. Erhard, for instance, availed himself of every possible opportunity to express his views on this point.

The partisans of a new agreement, however, met with strong resistance—from the "Europeans," first of all, who did not wish to see their great victory, the creation of the Common Market, compromised. For them, the Treaty of Rome was untouchable. Any attempt to amend it would compromise irremediably the work to which they had devoted their careers. And in France, the business interests who, in return for their support of the Common Market idea, had acquired strong positions behind its customs barriers, were not ready to risk the competition of an open market. Nor did the French Government encourage them to do so. In the Europe of the Six, France enjoyed great influence; she was a major catalytic agent, and it was a political opportunity she intended to use. In the absence of Great Britain, which had left the field open, De Gaulle concentrated his efforts on the strengthening of Franco-German collaboration, in the avowed hope of re-establishing the balance of power within the Atlantic Alliance, a goal made possible by the European unity created with and around France.

The United States, furthermore, supported the Common Market. It was not that she unconditionally approved of De Gaulle's ideas—quite the contrary. It appeared to Americans that his increasing opposition to U.S. preponderance in NATO, and his military policy—which, by developing an independent French nuclear striking force, aimed at giving France greater independence from her allies—compromised the integration efforts carried on in NATO. But the Treaty of Rome was in line with American policy as it had developed ever since the Marshall Plan. If the United States supported the Europe of the Six against the Europe of the Seven, it was not because Common Market propaganda and lobbies were more powerful than those of the EFTA or because Jean Monnet's influence in Washington was so considerable, but rather because she approved of its political objectives. To the United States, European political union seemed both necessary and desirable.

The economic success of the EEC did, however, cause her some worries, for she risked being excluded from a valuable protected European market. It was possible that the free-trade orientation of the EFTA would be more favorable to her in the last analysis. These issues were all the more urgent as the economic situation of the United States deteriorated. The recession that had set in during the spring of 1960 was particularly striking in contrast to Europe's brilliant economic expansion, and it had come closely on the heels of the 1958 recession, from which the economy had not yet fully recovered. "The present state of our economy is disturbing," declared President Kennedy in his first State of the Union Message on January 30, 1961. "We take office in the wake of seven months of recession, three and one half years of economic slack, seven years of diminished economic growth, and nine years of falling farm income." (Eisenhower's last message to the Congress, eighteen days earlier, although less pessimistic, had nonetheless recognized the existence of "intermittent slowdowns" and unemployment at a level higher than desirable.)

The deficit in the balance of payments also caused the Administration increasing worry. The President remarked that this deficit had grown by nearly $11 billion since 1958, and that a net loss of about $5 billion of the gold reserves had resulted, despite rather substantial trade surpluses. The subse-

quent analysis of this deficit led to a wide-ranging debate on
the components of American power and on the nature of the
U.S. role in the postwar world: the importance of governmental expenditures for the support of American troops sta-
tioned abroad and for economic and military aid to allies or
underdeveloped regions; the increasing flight of private capital due in part to the establishment of foreign subsidiaries and
in part to the obvious advantages of investment in Europe;
and, lastly, the effect of Europe's rapid economic development, which threatened American competitors in the world
market, handicapped as they were by restrictive regulations
and noncompetitive prices.

But the realization of these factors did not induce the
American Government to modify its attitude in regard to the
European Economic Community. In remarkably precise
terms, they sketched out a form of collaboration with the new
Europe—a united, strong European partner. After years of
putting the brake on efforts to develop nonmilitary collaboration within the NATO framework, the American Government in reaction against the centrifugal forces that French
military policy and the creation of new poles of European
integration had encouraged, reverted to the Atlantic theme.
But it was not within NATO that the attempt to strengthen
the ties between Europe and America would be made. The
OEEC, whose worth was universally acknowledged and
which was the one remaining bridge between the two Europes, became the focal point for this policy. Rather than
dissolve the OEEC—which some thought had fulfilled its
mission but which nonetheless retained a symbolic value during this period of crisis—a means was sought to adapt it to
the new situation created by the establishment of the Common
Market and the EFTA, by the renewed convertibility of most
European currencies, by the desire in the United States and
Canada to strengthen economic ties with Europe, and by the
need (recognized on all sides) to give priority to the problems

of the developing countries. The initiative had been taken at the end of 1959, at the time of the Paris Summit Conference, and it led, one year later, to the convention setting up the Organization for Economic Cooperation and Development, which in addition to the members of the old OEEC, also included Canada and the United States. The OECD charged itself, according to one pacifying formula, with those activities necessary to the "continuity of cooperation in the fields where no change is called for."* Although one of the purposes of the new organization was to "contribute to the expansion of world trade on a multilateral, nondiscriminatory basis in accordance with international obligations," and although the members were asked to "pursue their efforts to reduce or abolish obstacles to the exchange of goods and services,"† the OECD's principal mission was the support of the developing countries.

The creation of the OECD had not ended the division of Europe: It had simply kept alive an instrument of economic cooperation whose policy was now more closely in tune with American preoccupations. The two Europes continued to face one another in unequal combat. The EFTA, whose open-door policy might appear more in accord with the traditional concept of a Europe "without shores" spreading throughout the world, was nevertheless unable to fight against the power of the European myth. The forms of economic cooperation it recommended, valid as they might be, seemed too classic to a world in love with change. Worst still, to a continent that had felt its very existence threatened for decades, it offered no genuine new policy. How was Europe to face up to the growing threat of the Soviet Union? True, the Euro-

* See the resolution voted on January 13, 1960, by the ministers of thirteen countries, in *A Remodelled Economic Organisation: A Report by the Group of Four* (Paris, April, 1960), p. 8.

† Convention on the Organisation for Economic Cooperation and Development of December 14, 1960 (Paris, 1960), Articles 1, 2.

pean Economic Community did not give a direct answer either to this question, but it showed a will to regroup; it showed where to seek a solution, in which direction to move; it took a definite step into the future. The EFTA, on the other hand, lacked a banner to symbolize its European convictions.

In the EFTA, which respected (even cultivated) differences, and which grouped together states scattered in the four corners of Europe, Great Britain played a decisive role. Now, forces favorable to a *rapprochement* with the Common Market were relatively powerful in Great Britain, and they continued to gain strength. The spectacular recovery of the European economy seemed most impressive at a moment when the British economy appeared to be incapable of overcoming its chronic difficulties. The Common Market had stimulated the European economic organism, especially the French, and the English had the greatest need of a stimulant. Moreover, on whom could Great Britain count in this economic and political struggle? The support the United States was giving to the Common Market had reduced the value of the special community of English-speaking nations; changes had altered the Commonwealth's substance and spirit and it had become more a burden than a support. And the other members of the EFTA could hardly serve as counterweights to the continental power of the Common Market.

Thus, at the very moment when the EFTA was beginning to get organized, there developed a movement favorable to Britain's signing of the Treaty of Rome. Governments, of course, remained silent. But the British decision in July, 1960, to transfer responsibility for the conduct of European affairs from Maudling to Heath (i.e., from the Board of Trade and the Treasury to the Foreign Office) was more than a mere shuffle of men and offices. As early as the autumn of 1960, the British Government, without altering its membership in various alliances, was in the process of preparing for a radical change in its European policy.

While the Europeans argued over the modalities of integration, a new threat came to the fore. In early November, 1958, Khrushchev had publicly reopened the Berlin problem, dormant since the Blockade. His first speech—it was conceived and executed as an ultimatum—left little room for doubt as to his real intentions. Khrushchev addressed himself to the Western powers as a man conscious of the immense power at his command and as a man ready to use it. But his self-assurance did not depend uniquely on the conviction that Soviet affairs were firmly in his hands or on the successes of Soviet science and technology: There probably also was his knowledge of the weaknesses of his Western opponents. He knew that the Soviet Union had overwhelming superiority in conventional armaments, which adversaries could surmount only by resorting to nuclear weapons—that is to say, only by instigating and taking responsibility for a conflict they did not want. He also knew that a Western operation to "disengage" Berlin implied an offensive undertaking on NATO's part, for which the public, accustomed to think of NATO as an exclusively defensive alliance, was not prepared. Neither was he ignorant of the discussions that NATO members had been holding for years in full public view: over the free trade zone and Franco-British rivalry in it, over Algeria, over the difficulties of scientific cooperation, and over the policy of "disengagement" and Great Britain's reluctance to support Dulles' and Adenauer's position. He was aware of the American malaise caused by the weakness of her leader, he knew France's difficulties, he was well informed on the ups and downs of British foreign policy and on the growing temptation, on the eve of the elections, for the two rival parties to outbid each other as proponents of "peace."

As for the German Federal Republic, whose interests would be most directly affected by a Berlin settlement, she seemed neither as strong nor as resolute as she had been a few years earlier. Chancellor Adenauer still exercised uncontested power, despite his age, and it was to him that the Christian Democratic Union (CDU) owed its victory in the 1957 elections. Every aspect of government work was focused around him, all essential decisions depended on him, especially those that concerned foreign policy. Adenauer was not a man to change a policy that seemed successful to him. Thanks to him, Germany had again taken up its place in Europe and among the Atlantic nations. She was reconciled with France, bound to her by solid ties and common interests. She had gained the confidence of the United States. And more important, the Federal Republic had regained a degree of economic and financial power that impressed the Germans themselves, their allies, and the many nations throughout the world who were in need of capital and goods. She was, more than France or Great Britain, in a position to offer substantial support to the European cause. Beside her, the German Democratic Republic, dragging along in the wake of Russian policy and maintained only through the will of the U.S.S.R., looked mediocre indeed. Everyone who had the opportunity to visit both parts of Germany, everyone who went from West to East Berlin, was struck by the difference in the respective standards of living, a difference underscored by the daily exodus of East Germans seeking better living conditions and the freedom refused them by a regime made all the more oppressive because of its fragility.

But neither the "economic miracle" nor the political recovery of the Federal Republic had given it the stability and guarantee of continuity to which it aspired. Chancellor Adenauer's Germany remained the Germany of Bonn, weighted down by its division from the East and still inspired by the hope—more or less intense—of reunification. The Chancellor, aware of the difficulties and probably convinced of the uselessness of negotiation, had not directed his efforts toward that goal. On the contrary, he had turned to the West and, with obstinate perseverance, had labored to bind Germany ever more closely to Western Europe and her powerful American ally. Only in this way, he thought, could Germany's position be consolidated and favorable conditions created for negotiation leading to reunification. Yet this strategy had helped to make the division of his country even clearer and to render all the more difficult the interchange and "osmosis" that might have paved the way for future unification. Was another policy possible? Those who argued for alternative lines of action perhaps underestimated the effect of the steps the Soviet Union had taken immediately after her victory in her zone of occupation. From the very first, the division had been made, and the monetary reform—upon which West Germany's economic and political recovery had depended—had only consecrated it. From the beginning, Germany was caught up in a web of contradictions; in those circumstances, the chasm could not fail to widen and the rivalry between the two Germanys to intensify. Under such conditions, the solution depended on the balance of power.

In the winter of 1958–59, that balance of power was not as favorable to the German Federal Republic as Chancellor Adenauer would have wished. The value and efficacy of Germany's alliance with the West was a function of the power and the resolution of the allies, and at the moment, they were uncertain and divided. In addition, Adenauer was facing increasing domestic opposition. Given the Federal Republic's exposed situation, the agreement of parties on a common foreign-policy program was necessary. In Austria, for example, the People's Party and the Social Democratic Party had for many years found it essential to relegate their doctrinal differences to the background in order to safeguard the country's independence and integrity in the face of an external threat. This was not the case in Germany, where the Christian Democrats and Socialists had tried to maintain their independence and freedom of action. The struggle that had ensued had grown more and more bitter, the adversaries less and less inclined to conciliation. The late Socialist leader Kurt Schumacher had made the debate an impassioned one from the very beginning; Adenauer, a real fighter, would not seek appeasement. His advancing years, far from inclining him to serenity, hardened him into intransigence. Since he intended to lead the fight himself, it was around his person and his policy that the battle was fought. What the Social Democrats attacked him for, first of all, was his permanent hold on power, the overwhelming personal influence he exercised that constantly assured his party a majority in the Bundestag. Three times, in 1949, 1953, and 1957, he had led his party to victory, keeping the SPD in an opposition that became less and less bearable for them. They attacked his methods of government, the personal character of his politics, so incompatible, they said, with a truly democratic regime. The Chancellor's authoritarianism was criticized all the more frequently as the impatience of his lieutenants in the CDU became known.

But most of all, his foreign policy came under attack. As far as the government's domestic policies were concerned, the SPD could not but be silenced by the "economic miracle," achieved in spite of their dire predictions of disaster. They might criticize the *Soziale Marktwirtschaft* or refuse to recognize the beneficial social effects attributed to it by its proponents, but they were put in an embarrassing position when asked to define their own socialist political economy. Like all socialist parties in Western Europe, they were going through an ideological crisis and no longer believed, as they had before the war, that socialization of the means of production was a panacea for all ills. They satisfied themselves with insisting on the necessity of a more equitable distribution of goods and with the importance of finding methods and styles adapted to the new industrial revolution, to the modern era of great scientific discoveries. It was an extremely moderate program, all in all, which forced the SPD to moderation in its criticisms;

it wanted to be listened to, after all, in a society where the middle class was constantly growing.

In foreign policy, however, there were opportunities to be taken that would make up for losses in domestic affairs. And in that sphere, there were themes that would naturally arouse an emotional response in any audience: the divided Germany, atomic death, the danger of alliances. The Socialists did not miss their chance. With all the passion of their great leader Schumacher, whose influence continued after his death, they carefully followed the Chancellor's every action and appointed themselves guardians of the German heritage against a policy that seemed to them to subordinate the interests of the nation to those of Europe. They stood against concessions to France in the Saar and were appeased only after the return of that province to the German fatherland. In every way, they sought to put a brake on the Federal Republic's evolution toward the Atlantic world. It was not that they were opposed in principle to the construction of Europe: some Social Democrats, like Professor Carlo Schmid, were active European militants. But they feared that one effect would be to reinforce Soviet control over the German Democratic Republic and thus formalize the division of Germany. In fact, although the SPD was scarcely disposed to make concessions on the eastern frontiers of Germany—this was a theme on which both parties exercised prudence, for fear of furnishing the other with a means of getting votes—they continued to hope that negotiations with the U.S.S.R. would be possible. The Federal Republic and the Western powers, they repeated incessantly, had committed a grave error in 1952, in refusing almost out of hand a Soviet initiative on the reunification of Germany under acceptable conditions. They had preferred to take the road to rearmament, and that had brought Germany to the present impasse. It was therefore important to seize every opportunity for military disengagement, in order to create the relaxation that was necessary to any resumption of negotiations.

Khrushchev's reopening of the Berlin issue, therefore, fell
on fertile ground. At first, it had provoked a lively and almost
unanimously negative reaction, but the time set in the ultimatum of November 27 was long enough (six months) to
allow all sides time for reflection. Khrushchev's alternate
threats and appeals to reason, blows and caresses, were cleverly
aimed to encourage a debate in both the United States and
Western Europe, in the course of which the differences in
outlook and in the choice of strategies would become progressively sharper.

It was the kind of test the Western allies were in no condition to withstand. If it had been a matter of a classic ultimatum
supported by a show of force, unity within NATO would
have been established rapidly and the defense organized immediately. But the military threat was an indirect one. Just
perceptible enough to create anxiety and a feeling of urgency,
it was carefully presented in such a way as to avoid provoking
an inflexible retaliation. The entire operation had a political
character, aimed at imposing negotiation on the Atlantic allies,
who until then had refused any such proposal and who, everyone knew, disagreed on what the objectives and nature of the
negotiation should be.

Their first reflex had been to refuse the opportunity for
discussion which the Russian ultimatum offered. But the
awareness of the risks involved, and the pressure of public
opinion dominated by fear of an atomic catastrophe, had
forced them to alter this negative response. The governments
of these Western democracies do not dispose of the freedom
of action their opponent seems to enjoy. Far from being able
to work in silence and secrecy, they are daily assaulted by
advice from the public or from those who claim to speak in its
name. Whatever they may say or do, they are in constant
danger of being caught in the stream of commentaries, interpretations, contradictory suggestions, and carried along in a
direction they do not wish to follow by a current of opinions

that has gained strength from its anonymity. Prime Minister Macmillan, like Adenauer in the Federal Republic, knew that the opposition had been won over to a policy of "disengagement." Nor could the United States afford intransigeance when the issue was a primarily European crisis without running the risk of alienating a substantial part of European public opinion.

In Germany, the Social Democratic Party, making another sacrifice to their policy of reunification, proposed a plan for an "all-German commission based on parity" (*Gesamtdeutsche Konferenz auf der Grundlage der Parität*), and for a "relaxation-of-tension zone" (*Entspannungszone*) including the two parts of Germany, Poland, Czechoslovakia, and Hungary, which would lead to the withdrawal of those regions from the security systems of which they were now a part.

The allies also allowed themselves to be caught up in the meshes of blackmail. Macmillan, knowing the sensitivity of British public opinion on the subject of atomic war and facing an election campaign, made a virtue of necessity and took it upon himself to go on a "reconnaissance" mission to Moscow early in 1959. Would this lead to a new Munich? Political confusion in the West was such that the question did come up. But what Macmillan brought back from his trip was a suspension of the deadline in return for the opening of negotiations. Consequently, the summer of 1959 went by in somewhat more relaxed discussions. The failure of the Foreign Ministers' Conference did not prevent other contacts. In Moscow, Richard Nixon began his campaign for the Presidency of the United States during a visit that was the prelude to Khrushchev's American tour in the fall of 1959.

But the idyll did not last long. The new negotiations in preparation for the Summit Conference came to naught. The U-2 incident in the spring of 1960 came just at the right moment to allow Khrushchev, with a flood of threats and insolent remarks, to break up the negotiations from which he could in any event gain nothing.

The Berlin crisis receded. Europeans and their Atlantic allies could enjoy a new respite. For how long, they did not know. Despite their renewed prosperity, despite the brilliant new economic prospects that seemed to be opening up, anxiety persisted throughout Europe, and in the United States as well, where the President seemed more and more to have been left behind by events, his term of office ending in a series of humiliating defeats.

"Peace through terror" cannot furnish that tranquillity of mind without which life finally becomes unbearable. Everyone knew that the atomic balance was unstable, that it could be destroyed either by the enlargement of the nuclear club or by modification in the use or nature of atomic missiles. The advantage the U.S.S.R. seemed to have in intercontinental missiles was cause for reflection: More and more, the Europeans asked with General de Gaulle whether the American Government would be ready to take on the formidable responsibility for the loss of millions of American lives in order to live up to its commitments on other continents. The price of collective security was becoming so high that one hesitated to believe it could be paid.

❦[9]❦

1961: A Year of Crisis

The year 1960 ended under difficult conditions for the West. France was encumbered by her Algerian war; Germany was still divided; England was impoverished and resigned; the lessening of Presidential authority in the United States had led to utter confusion; Khrushchev seemed to dominate the world political scene. Already he was sounding the victory trumpet, inviting the vast coalition of Sovietized peoples, Communist parties, and dependent or semidependent countries to divide among them the remnants of capitalist imperialism. In November, 1960, the representatives of all the Communist and Workers' parties of the world had published a long declaration containing this significant passage:

> Today it is the world socialist system and the forces fighting against imperialism for a socialist transformation of society that determine the main content, main trend, and main features of the historical development of society. Whatever efforts imperialism makes, it cannot stop the advance of history. A reliable basis has been provided for further decisive victories for socialism. The complete triumph of socialism is inevitable.*

* Declaration of Representatives of the Eighty-one Communist Parties (Moscow Conference of November-December, 1960), in *The New Communist Manifesto and Related Documents* (2nd ed.; Evanston, Ill.: Row, Peterson, 1962), p. 12.

In the United States, President Kennedy, after getting acquainted with the problems he had inherited, admitted to his fellow countrymen that these were difficult times. "No man entering upon this office," he said in his State of the Union Message of 1961, "regardless of his party, regardless of his previous service in Washington, could fail to be staggered upon learning—even in this brief ten-day period—the harsh enormity of the trials through which we must pass in the next four years. Each day the crises multiply. Each day their solution grows more difficult. Each day we draw nearer the hour of maximum danger, as weapons spread and hostile forces grow stronger. I feel that I must inform the Congress that our analyses over the last ten days make it clear that, in each of the principal areas of crisis, the tide of events has been running out and time has not been our friend."

President Kennedy lacked neither courage nor the spirit of enterprise. On the contrary. But he could not rest on his laurels, and, having come to office after a forcefully fought personal battle, he had now to demonstrate that he was worthy of his victory. He knew he was capable of that demonstration; he had not entered the fray by chance. Like all men of great ambition, Kennedy was calculating. His conquest of the Presidency was the fruit of long reflection and the triumph of a campaign whose organization had revealed a real mastery of political techniques. The same methodical procedures characterized the way in which he drew up the Administration program. The problems were systematically studied and the most varied opinions sought. The new President belonged to a generation for whom the future had already begun, but he kept his feet on the ground. He knew the weight of the responsibilities he was taking on and he understood what was at stake. From all this there came that mixture of boldness and caution that was his hallmark.

His choice of colleagues was revealing, not so much because of the large influx of intellectuals, but because of the proportion between organizers and "thinkers." Kennedy surrounded himself with thoughtful and imaginative men, but he did not forget the need for action. In all, his Administration was one of the most brilliant the United States could assemble. Kennedy had the advantage over his predecessor in being able to recruit men with experience not only in business administration but also in the politics of affairs of state. There were those who had been in the Truman Administration, and who had continued to keep abreast of events; there were many professors —historians, economists, sociologists, and political scientists— who had closely studied the problems the government had to resolve; and there were various members of the old Republican Administration.

As for the program, it was marked by the wish to strike the imagination and be reassuring at the same time. Kennedy appealed, with his admirable theme of the "New Frontier," to the pioneer spirit. The wish was to shake up the American people, to awaken their spirit of enterprise, to employ their unremitting optimism in the service of the great tasks posed by a world in the midst of revolution. This did not mean entering into some grand adventure. No, on the contrary, the goal that Kennedy proposed to the American people, the objective of those efforts he hoped they would make, was security. The point was to demonstrate to oneself—and thereby also to those other nations threatened by totalitarianism— that it was possible to ensure individual peace and security in a land of freedom. Kennedy had set himself the goal of following Roosevelt.

But his task was infinitely more difficult. Roosevelt had come to power at a moment of national crisis, carried to office on a great groundswell of public opinion. With such support, he enjoyed great freedom of action. Kennedy, on the other hand, had to reckon with a formidable opposition of conservative Democrats and right-wing Republicans. Public opinion, disoriented as it was, was unaware of the gravity of the international situation and of the special nature of the war in which America and the West were pitted against the Soviet offensive. Attention was focused on problems of domestic politics, and international politics infringed on the daily life of the average American only infrequently, at times of acute crisis.

How was Kennedy to make this numbed and enervated America accept the New Frontier? How was he to win over American society, increasingly fixed and stratified, to a quasi-revolutionary program? Not many understood that the renewal of effort urged by the young President was aimed—through the amelioration of the living conditions of the American people—at strengthening the international position and influence of the United States. For the most part, that is, for everyone who had misunderstood the political character of the Cold War, every social reform was a concession to socialism that would lead to the weakening of the traditional structure of American society and therefore of its capacity to resist. Kennedy found this argument used constantly by the conservative coalition; the increasing threats of a military conflict, far from facilitating his task, only strengthened these reactionary tendencies.

The militants of the New Frontier found it difficult, then, to communicate their enthusiasm to the American people. Their reforming zeal met with a skeptical Congress, which calmly absorbed the shock of Kennedy's successive messages and continued on its piecemeal destruction of the Presidential program. At the end of the year, the Democratic Administration could take pride in certain successes, it was true. Business had picked up; the gold outflow had been much reduced, if not stopped; unemployment had dropped; public-opinion polls showed a rise in the President's popularity. But Kennedy had been unable to attain the break-through he had hoped for. Some of his greatest projects—medical aid for the aged, the modernization and advancement of the educational establishment, youth-training programs—had been opposed in the

Congress; the GNP at the end of 1961 was $516 billion, but the growth rate of the American economy was still low; many industries were still functioning below capacity; certain regions had not yet felt the effects of the recovery; the total number of unemployed was still rather high, at 7 per cent of the active civilian population. Satisfied as Americans were with the long-term effects of the Marshall Plan, their admiration for the economic recovery of Europe was nonetheless tempered with not a little envy and anxiety when they considered their own situation at the end of 1961.

In the international field, the balance sheet for the year was scarcely more encouraging. The legacy of the Republican Administration was singularly burdensome: crises in Latin America, where "Fidelism" was making many converts; crises in Southeast Asia, where the war in Laos threatened the West's last allies on the Indochinese peninsula and divided SEATO; crises in United States-Japanese relations; crises in NATO; and crises in the United Nations. The system of pacts and alliances established to contain the advance of the Soviet Union was breaking down under the pressures of nationalism and contradictory interests. And the great world organization —designed to assure the security of each of its members—was torn by internal rivalries and kept alive only by the political intelligence and moral authority of its Secretary General.

The new American Administration strove to right the situation with a will to assume the full responsibilities implicit in the restoration of American leadership. The problems were not new, and the Administration was prepared to face them. The objective was simple enough: It was a matter of reversing the current of events, of taking the West off the defensive and seizing the initiative once again. America and her allies must have their confidence restored, their shaken alliances tightened; the ideals of the New Frontier must be communicated to the non-Communist world by furnishing proof of their worth. The United States, for the second time in the twentieth century, hoped to show the way to economic and social progress and peace, not only to Europe but to the new Asian and African states. To the United Nations, a token of her sincerity was offered in the form of almost unconditional support. To the Soviet Union, the prospect of a relaxation of tension was offered through renewed negotiations on arms control. Not that the Administration had illusions about the real objectives of Soviet policy. But the new President and his advisers could not help realizing, as many specialists on nuclear policy did also, that the Soviet leaders must be as conscious as they of the folly of atomic war. A convergence of interests, the first condition for fruitful negotiations, might be born of their common peril.

In sum, there was little that was new in this program, except the manner of its presentation and the style of the Administration that offered it: a mixture of youthful fervor and high seriousness.

But, just at the moment when the new Administration had gained momentum and, as it were, taken flight, an accident stopped it cold. In a situation so full of risks, an error in calculation was always possible: Here, the miscalculation concerned Cuba. The first measures taken by President Kennedy, though, had revealed his plan to maneuver around this obstacle to his Latin American policies. The message of March 13 proposing a ten-year plan for economic and social development in Latin America, the Alliance for Progress, struck at what was thought to be the root of the evil. But it was a long-term remedy whose merits Fidel Castro—as always cleverly exploiting each and every occasion for propaganda purposes—naturally attributed to himself. His intervention could not fail to complicate and retard, if not actually prevent, the urgent recovery program, and in any case, his revolutionary island threatened the security of the United States and the Western Hemisphere. A number of Americans considered the overthrow of Castro's regime essential. But in order to make this possible,

U.S. military support was required. Kennedy allowed himself
to be convinced of the necessity of the operation while refusing to those who undertook it the American military cover
they demanded. The resulting failure was a considerable blow
to the prestige of the United States. Still, if it had been a military error, it was not a totally erroneous political move. The
very fact that Castro was victorious furnished proof that the
President of the United States had avoided imposing publicly
a policy that contradicted the principle of self-determination.
Both in the United States and in Latin America, that was
something to be grateful for.

Nonetheless, the Bay of Pigs affair caused trouble. Inevitably,
it furnished grist to the anti-Yankee imperialism propaganda
mill; it tempered enthusiasm in the new Administration and
reduced its confidence. The Administration had been misin-
formed and had sinned through excessive optimism. Some of
its members, who should have been able to furnish a valid
evaluation of the military and political situation regardless,
had made disturbing errors in judgment; experience would
lead to prudence. But above all, the Bay of Pigs venture once
more revealed the limits on the freedom of action of a great
world power. If the United States wished to see the nations of
Latin America reject "Fidelism," which firmly placed its supporters in the socialist camp led by the Soviet Union, the
United States could do nothing but supply ever-increasing
economic aid, the efficacy of which she could not be sure. At
most—and this was to be an essential point in the Alliance for
Progress Charter of Punta del Este—she could make the grant
of aid conditional on the establishment of an economic development program and of reforms in the recipient country. But
she had no means of actual control over the way the funds
were used, still less of ensuring political stability, which was
the precondition for any real development. At the end of
1961, Castro was still a threat, frustrating the continued efforts

for moderation on the part of the United States and Latin American governments.

The United States found herself in just as poor, if not worse, a situation in Southeast Asia, for the war in Laos was turning against her, for what reasons it was difficult to say. Some accused "the ugly American"; others held the intervention of the North Vietnamese responsible. Whatever the origins of the new crisis, it was evident to American policymakers that their freedom of action was limited here as well. In this factional war, the elements favorable to the United States were not making good use of either their military superiority or political astuteness. To redress the balance, however, would require American commitments quite disproportionate to the strategic importance of the region, made under the skeptical and critical eye of French and English allies. But neither could they give in without running the risk of compromising Thailand's position and the safety of South Vietnam, and consequently of losing all Indochina. Faced with the impossibility of settling matters once and for all, compromise solutions were sought, only to end up in the paradox that the West was forced to accept a solution that delivered it up to its enemies, while at the very same moment it was decided to go all out in the war of the two Vietnams.

On the European side of the Atlantic, the political situation among members of the Atlantic Alliance during 1961 was not much more encouraging.

The United Kingdom moved laboriously ahead under a government whose prestige had already declined. The men in Macmillan's government were far from being incapable, and some (particularly the younger members) had, through their competence and their conviction, pushed to the fore. But these qualities had been used more often to negotiate new "honorable" retreats. Could it have been otherwise? Great Britain's might, once so feared, seemed to have been reduced, her governmental tasks limited to the progressive liberation of England from "the white man's burden" and the obligation of power. This was a difficult maneuver, nonetheless, pitting those colonists who had once been England's pride and a steady source of her wealth against the government, without winning the gratitude of those whom England was helping to make the delicate transition from colonial status to independence. Because the road was long and the possible obstacles many—in Kenya; in Rhodesia; in the Union of South Africa, whose break with the Commonwealth had not freed England of the burden that the solidarity of the white race put on her; in the Middle East, where great economic interests were at stake; in the Indian Peninsula, where the Kashmir conflict was still an issue (not to mention Goa, where Great Britain had resigned herself to sacrificing an old European ally on the altar of anticolonialism)—each stage in the retreat required new choices, painful and humiliating ones, which exacerbated old quarrels and gave rise to sterile anger that was dissipated in a gray fog of the struggle for daily existence.

In a world imbalanced by scientific discoveries and technical transformations, England, which lacked neither scholars nor political thinkers, seemed to hesitate, playing for time, hoping to see the crises lose their virulence and to avoid impossible choices. But the other nations were advancing, their ardor growing with the hopes and risks they saw before them. The Soviet thrust was becoming more imperious, the nationalism of the new states more aggressive, the Common Market more dynamic, the United States more pressing. Yet Great Britain no longer had even the means to play the honest broker, a role to which she had resigned herself for lack of anything better. Thus, and this was the great decision of the year, she turned toward Europe. The revision of the European policy of Great Britain, which had begun with the ministerial reshuffle of July, 1960, ended in August, 1961, with Macmillan's announcement of his decision to open negotiations on British adherence to the Treaty of Rome.

If Great Britain was not in a position to lead the way, did this mean that France was? General de Gaulle thought so, and statistics confirmed the optimistic surveys he periodically presented to his fellow countrymen during 1961: growth in industrial production, growth in foreign commerce, rising wages, a favorable state of public finances, surplus in the balance of payments. France was advancing full steam ahead.

But the war in Algeria was not over. For a while, it had been possible to believe that the government had the situation well in hand: The referendum of January 8 had given it a majority in favor of settling the conflict; the April "generals' rebellion" had been abortive. But negotiations with the Provisional Algerian Government had produced no results, despite the conferences at Evian and Lugrin. De Gaulle was caught between two extremist adversaries locked in mortal combat, and he seemed to be losing control of the situation. In order to negotiate, and especially in order to agree to "Algerian Algeria," he needed support, which the majority of the nation accorded him, but which the Europeans in Algeria, the Army officers, and certain elements in the government bureaucracy refused him. This weakness encouraged the leaders of the FLN to stiffen their demands in order to obtain from the outset that full independence of all Algerian territory that the French Government wished to grant them only after a certain lapse of time. Supported by international public opinion and by part of the French public, and protected from military intervention at their foreign bases, they were convinced that time was on their side. The successive concessions to which France consented only strengthened this conviction. But it was also true that these very concessions and the prolongation of the conflict stimulated a resistance to the granting of independence and gave it time to organize: The OAS men who threw plastic bombs answered the FLN terrorists; Algeria was

sliding into anarchy. The French Government still had juridical power there—with its army, police force, and administration. But these agents of the state were powerless.

Anarchy spread to Metropolitan France, where the plastic
bombs were set off almost daily. The OAS, although not
powerful, had well-placed allies. The fact that it presented
itself as the defender of a national cause gained it both sympathy and actual cooperation; its anonymous terrorism allowed
it to exploit the weak. The government tried to prevent this,
but its efforts were weak and inconsistent. Careful to avoid
being pushed along the path to dictatorship, but having to
enforce order, it was satisfied with half-measures that only
disconcerted the public. Contradictory criticisms were loudly
voiced on all sides. The free press was used to voice opposition
to government sanctions, while simultaneously the government was reproached for not knowing how to make its authority respected. It went its own way with an irritating blindness to these criticisms, apparently deaf to advice as well. And
its enemies were many—on the left, on the right, in the Assembly and Senate, in the unions, among intellectuals, in the
rural areas. France was prosperous, no doubt, but the French,
or at least those who claimed to speak in their name, believed
they had cause for complaint, even the right to deny the state
their obedience. The government had undertaken too many
reforms, touched on too many problems, put too many forces
into motion. Now it was reproached for being guilty of both
excessive audacity and timidity.

Apparently imperturbable in the midst of this chaos, General de Gaulle found reason for hope in the advances made
thanks to the re-establishment of state authority. He did not
underestimate the strength he drew from the exercise of legitimate power vis-à-vis his divided adversaries. But his self-
imposed isolation reduced the possibilities of action, both
within the country and beyond its frontiers, and made it all

the more difficult to guarantee that continuity of power he considered essential after his departure.

Thus did the Algerian crisis compromise France's brilliant economic recovery. It divided the nation and kept it from assuming the international responsibilities its geographical position entailed, and at the very moment when a still more serious crisis was brewing, a crisis that threatened to destroy both NATO and the European structure.

For Khrushchev had once again raised the question of Berlin. But this time, he was not content with threats and declarations of intent; he took action. Why did he reactivate this issue after having let it lie quiescent since the spring of 1960? Why did he repeat the ultimatum at his very first meeting with the new President of the United States, just when the Kennedy Administration, in discussions on disarmament and on Laos, was showing its desire to seek a *modus vivendi* acceptable to both camps? Was it because Khrushchev wanted to protect the Soviet Union against the threat of German militarism, as the Soviet Government claimed? Or was it more simply a matter of wanting to consolidate the German Democratic Republic, which could no longer tolerate a permanent confrontation of the two systems? It was probable that both these considerations played a role in the Soviet decision, for the instability of Ulbricht's regime was a constant source of trouble within the Soviet alliance system in Eastern Europe.

But this defensive reasoning was a tactical move in a clearly offensive strategic maneuver. By bringing up the Berlin issue again, Khrushchev was once more seeking to disturb the Western alliance. Conscious of Soviet power, he wished to force the "imperialists" to recognize that the power relationships had been modified. The prestige of the Soviet Union, he said, demanded that its wishes be taken into account. The abandonment of Berlin by the Western powers, or at least the transformation of its status, the direct or indirect recognition of the German Democratic Republic—all these concessions were to be a demonstration of the changes in power relationships, the more evident because granted under Soviet pressure. Once proof had been furnished that the United States and her European allies would shrink back from this test of strength, and that they would easily abandon a few thousand Berliners whom they had promised protection, it would be more than probable that the West Germans would show less interest in Atlantic or European cooperation.

What could the Western powers do in the face of this public challenge? A pure and simple refusal to leave Berlin ran the risk of nuclear conflict. But the acceptance of Soviet conditions for remaining there would lead to a rift in the Atlantic Alliance and the fall of the West. There was no other solution but to stand up to the challenge and simultaneously to bring Khrushchev around to negotiations under conditions acceptable both to him and to the West. While the governments agreed on this essential point, their reactions were nonetheless marked (as they had been in 1959) by differences in temperament and situation. De Gaulle, conscious of the dangers of appearing to weaken under pressure of threats, refused to beg for negotiations, waiting instead for Khrushchev, who had after all initiated the crisis, to take the first steps. Macmillan, on the other hand, more sensitive than his French colleague to the pressure of public opinion and more naturally inclined to measures of compromises and procrastination, pushed for negotiations. Between the two, the American Administration, in which there were many contradictory currents of opinion, showed some hesitation. President Kennedy had made it clear both in Vienna and on his return to the United States that he would not shrink before such an attempt at intimidation. But he did not want to allow himself to be maneuvered by an enemy who he knew would seize any opportunity to put the responsibility for an open crisis on him. And he did not

wish to frighten his allies by too strong a reaction. He therefore tempered a spectacular reinforcement of the American
armed forces, which served to emphasize his determination,
with the affirmation that it was necessary to find a reasonable
solution, and with a delayed reaction to the construction of
the Berlin Wall and the implied acceptance of the *fait accompli*.

This Soviet operation, which had been carefully prepared,
could have been predicted. It was an obvious violation of the
spirit in which the status of Berlin had been agreed on and
was at the same time a provocative demonstration of strength.
But by cutting the city in two, the *Volkspolizei* of the D.D.R.
did not directly challenge the rights of the Western powers,
who retained the freedom to go from the Federal Republic
to West Berlin and to enter East Berlin. The Western governments, fearing even worse measures, resigned themselves to
abandoning the East Germans to their fate, while emphasizing
their intention, now strengthened in the new circumstances, to
honor their guarantee of support to West Berlin.

This decision obviously disappointed those in Germany
who had counted on a more vigorous Allied response. The
disappointment was great not only in East Germany, whose
inhabitants were henceforth prisoners of the Ulbricht regime,
but also in West Berlin, where it was naturally feared that this
retreat would lead to others. In the Federal Republic, which
the Berlin crisis had surprised in the midst of an election campaign, passions were deeply aroused. The government could
not intervene immediately in an affair that, juridically, concerned only the powers who had signed the agreements concerning the administration and control of Berlin. The caution
with which Chancellor Adenauer had to act was interpreted
by many of his compatriots, and especially the Berliners, as
a sign of weakness. Rightly or wrongly, the conclusion was
reached that his relation with the allies were unsure and consequently that a policy of firmness based on the Western

Alliance was now bankrupt. Various *faux pas* the old veteran made in regard to Willy Brandt raised the prestige of his rival, whom the Berlin crisis had naturally brought to the center of the stage. Adenauer saw arrayed against him not only his usual adversaries, but also some members of his own party who were uneasy at his growing authoritarianism. A great number of "floaters," who once had been responsive to his charm, were seeking another leader. It was for these reasons that the Christian Democratic Union lost its absolute majority. In the end, Adenauer kept his post as Chancellor, and thus his control over the foreign policy of the Federal Republic. But even if his personality still dominated the government coalition and reduced the effect of arrangements and agreements set up to remove him from power, his prestige was nonetheless hurt and the political stability of West Germany shaken.

By bowing to the *fait accompli* of the Berlin Wall, the allies had no doubt gained time. The stoppage of the exodus from East to West Germany, which had gravely threatened the very existence of the German Democratic Republic, allowed Khrushchev to take his time and to ignore his publicly announced schedule. But the success he thereby earned merely strengthened his confidence and encouraged him to pursue the investiture of this area. Rather than force the decision, with all the risks it included, it was just as worthwhile to weary the enemy and to gnaw away slowly at his defenses. The Wall was therefore reinforced and the number of check points reduced. Then, through a series of clever operations, the freedom of movement of allied personnel within Greater Berlin was restrained by presenting them with a choice between the presentation of an identity card to agents of the German Democratic Republic—which implied an indirect recognition of its right of control as a sovereign state—or giving up the right of passage. This measure was first applied to civilians, then extended to the military, and even, after various crises, to the American Commander in Chief in Berlin, who, in a reprisal measure directed at his Soviet colleague, himself contributed to the division of Berlin.

A propaganda campaign modeled on the successful campaign of 1959, accompanied this war of attrition, designed slowly to demoralize the population of the besieged city and to deprive it and its allied protectors of all reason to pursue a seemingly hopeless struggle. Soft words alternated with bellicose and provocative declarations, conciliatory measures with aggressive polemics.

The allies, united in their determination to stay in Berlin, were not in agreement on the means to reach this end, and their disagreements, given the defensive situation in which they had allowed themselves to be caught, only became more aggravated. Then, too, the Soviets could easily follow the development of their widely publicized discussions. Like everyone else, the Soviet leaders were *au courant* on all the changes in attitude, the tensions, and the differences of opinion. They knew not only the plans that the allies were thinking of submitting to them, but also all the various opinions on their advantages and disadvantages. They were supplied with virtually a whole spectrum of solutions to choose from. Some offered United Nations mediation, in both wholesale and retail versions. Other Westerners, who did not understand that one could risk war over the ex-capital of the odious Third Reich, were ready to accept the division the Soviets demanded and held tight to the magic formulas of "denuclearization" and "neutralization." Khrushchev did not lack Western spokesmen who were willing to help, either by reviving the debate or by orienting it in the direction he wished.

At the end of the year, it is true, the Western powers were still in Berlin under the military cover of demonstratively strengthened American forces, and Khrushchev could not ignore this. But Western freedom to maneuver had been curtailed by Allied disagreement over tactics and still more by the progressive narrowing of negotiable issues. It was no longer possible, as it had been at the beginning of the Summit Conference of 1955, to discuss the situation of the countries in Eastern Europe. It was no longer a matter of negotiating the conditions for reunifying Germany or even the status of Greater Berlin, but simply of knowing what would be the fate of the West Berliners. Colonel Soloviev, when he addressed General Watson in December as "the military governor of the American sector of West Berlin," revealed the distance that had been traveled.

In this Berlin crisis, so serious a threat to world peace, the United Nations should have been called upon to intervene. But the principal parties seemed to have agreed to keep the U.N. out of the matter. What could it have done in a conflict directly involving the leading members of the Security Council? For lack of sufficient tactical means, a certain moral authority would have had to suffice. But the United Nations was deeply affected by the revolutionary transformations taking place throughout the world. As the incarnation of the myth of world unity, all hope was centered on it. Called upon to show the new nations the road to progress and happiness, burdened with the most diverse political, economic, and military tasks, the U.N. had to affirm its presence everywhere at once: to localize a crisis, to train civil servants, to try to re-establish international bonds severed by nationalism. Now, the United Nations gathered together sovereign states that were incapable of abandoning their national ambitions and approaching problems without regard to particular interests, and that therefore carried their rivalries into the U.N. itself. The increased number of members, which was seen as a proof of the U.N.'s vitality and as a reason for hope, on the contrary contributed to a paralysis of the U.N. organism. Its achievements stood in inverse proportion to the increase in the number of its tasks.

Faced with world disorder that threatened to compromise the United Nations, Secretary General Dag Hammerskjöld had done his best to increase respect for the international civil service among his co-workers. But there was little time; successive world crises required rapid decisions. He had to accept help wherever he could find it, enlist whatever men were available, even if these men were not the best qualified or most conscientious civil servants. He had to recruit police forces and send them into action before they even had time to organize. And all this had to be done under the cross fire of criticisms and ever-growing controversy, without being able to count on the organization whose members could not even agree on the interpretation of its orders.

Thus, the upsurge of nationalism threatened to dislocate a magnificent and indispensable organization, created to assure peace in the world. Each member felt free to interpret the Charter as he wished and to limit his responsibilities accordingly. In the absence of agreement on fundamental principles, decisions were reached by virtue of chance majorities.

Here as elsewhere, Europe was cautious. Marked by her colonialist past, she remained nailed in the prisoner's dock. In vain she multiplied her concessions and bore active witness to her desire to proceed with systematic decolonization; she was nonetheless suspect as long as there remained a single dependent territory—that is to say, indefinitely. It was even argued that granting political independence did not end dependence as long as economic ties that bound together the advanced and underdeveloped countries remained, for this condition inevitably favored the advanced countries. According to this line of reasoning, aid to developing countries was only a manifestation of a neocapitalism as dangerous as the old colonial imperialism.

Consequently, anticolonial passion, far from calming down as progress was made in decolonization, seemed instead to become aggravated. Demographic pressures, economic difficulties, and internal political complications continually fed the nationalistic fervors directed against the last fragments of the colonial empires, but also against the "have" nations. And the attacks increased. India, losing patience, proceeded to conquer Goa, and the Security Council, blocked by the Soviet veto, could not stop this recourse to force. Indonesia refused to negotiate with Holland over anything but the pure and simple transfer of sovereignty over West Irian, and she openly proceeded to make preparations for war. The Egyptian Government compensated for the loss of prestige suffered because of the Syrian revolution by taking various policy measures aimed against Europe.

Against these assaults, the European nations were defenseless. They no longer had the strength to protect their interests and seemed paralyzed by a guilt complex. They could not count on United States support, for America was working to prevent the U.S.S.R. from turning the colonial revolt to its advantage. A strong current of opinion supported the demands based on self-determination vis-à-vis Europe. But outside of Europe, scarcely anyone was concerned over the right of the East Germans to determine their own fate in free elections. And the intervention of the Soviet Government in Finnish affairs gave rise to only timid protests.

It was understandable, then, that Khrushchev was as optimistic in December, 1961, as he had been in January. In his report to the Twenty-second Congress of the Communist Party of the Soviet Union, he recalled that the "chief content of the period following the Twentieth Congress of the CPSU was the competition of the two world social systems, the socialist and capitalist systems," and affirmed that "capitalism has been seriously cramped by socialism in a decisive sphere of human activity, that of material production," and that the socialist camp had sufficient military strength to defend itself against imperialist aggressors.

> In the years that have elapsed [since the Twentieth Congress], there have been further aggravation of contradictions both within the capitalist countries and between them. Colonial empires have been collapsing and the struggle of the working class and the national-liberation movement of the peoples have assumed huge proportions. The general tendency—the further decay of capitalism—has continued to operate ruthlessly.*

This optimism was reflected in the Third Party Program adopted by the CPSU. Between now and 1980, it affirmed:

> The material and technical basis of Communism will be built up . . . ensuring an abundance of material and cultural values for the whole population; Soviet society will come close to a stage where it can introduce the principle of distribution according to needs, and there will be a gradual transition to one form of ownership—public ownership. Thus, a Communist society will, in the main, be built in the U.S.S.R. The construction of Communist society will be fully completed in the subsequent period.†

And they went on to indicate, chapter by chapter, the objectives they proposed to reach: to augment the volume of industrial production by at least 600 per cent; to increase the over-all volume of agricultural production by 350 per cent; to suppress social, cultural, and economic differences between town and country; to reconcile centralized direction of the national economy with the development of the role and responsibility of federal and local organisms; to raise the standard of living by a two-pronged action designed to raise wages according to the quantity and quality of the work done and

* See N. S. Khrushchev, Documents of the Twenty-second Congress of the Communist Party of the Soviet Union (New York, 1961), Vol. I.
† "The Program of the Communist Party of the Soviet Union," *The New Communist Manifesto and Related Documents* (Evanston, Ill., 1962).

to increase the total amount of public funds distributed independently of the efforts of each individual; to increase the efficiency of the administration while democratizing it, in such a way as to prepare for the change-over of self-administration in Communist society, the precondition for the withering away of the state; to instill in each citizen a scientific conception of the world and respect for the "moral code of the Communist builder"; to strengthen the international proletariat and cooperation between the peoples of the world socialist system.

A magnificent program, in truth. But, behind the assurance, behind the repeated affirmations of Communism's superiority and the inevitability of its victory over capitalism, how many problems still faced those Soviet leaders!

There were economic problems. However great the progress made, the ambitious goals that had been set had not always been reached. One only has to look at the discrepancy between agricultural goals and actual harvests in China, or at Khrushchev's criticism of the agricultural administrators and workers in the U.S.S.R. Alone the estimates of the growth rate of Soviet agricultural production between 1950 and 1960 were cause for a skeptical appraisal of the possibilities of achieving the new program for the next twenty years, especially since the number of agricultural machines was still insufficient and the growth rate in fertilizer production noticeably smaller than that required by the plans. Observations of the rate of growth in industrial production also led to the conclusion that the law of diminishing returns was also applicable to socialist systems. In any case, these observations made it clear that the achievement of the Communist program implied not only continuing an already great effort, but also intensifying it. Moreover, it was impossible to maintain after observing the power of the United States and the brilliant economic recovery of Western Europe that the capitalist system was dying.

There were political problems. The Twenty-second Congress had been marked by a new crisis. Could one say that the battle was now over? What was the significance of the defeat of the Stalinists, of the "anti-Party group"? What would its consequences be? The relaxation of constraint is a necessary stage on the way to that withering away of the state postulated on the harmonization of individual wills. But the development of the critical spirit essential to the development of the personality may end in a radical questioning of the very foundation of Soviet society. How is this to be prevented, if not by maintaining a certain constraint, that is to say, by perpetuating the contradiction of means and ends? Similarly, it is difficult to reconcile centralized direction of the economy and social self-determination. Moreover, the Party, which holds effective power, tended to substitute itself for the state. To the extent that it would fulfill the mission assigned it in the Program, it would prepare for the withering away of the state, but not of state power, the prerogatives and functions of which it was taking over. Therefore, the Party, which included only an infinitesimal minority of the citizens, ran the risk of becoming a class by confounding itself with the state, of concretizing the very usurpation Marx condemned. The Soviet Union, whatever Khrushchev's claims or even hopes may have been, seemed to be inclining to an oligarchic society in which elected individuals, claiming socialist legitimacy, would control the state apparatus, now debaptized and called social self-administration. And the factional struggles, obvious substitutes for the party struggles within democratic regimes, went on, the loser condemned and cast from the Party in the name of a history whose determined course he had not known how to interpret.

Thus far we have considered only struggles within the Soviet state. But the Twenty-second Congress had revealed still more serious tensions in relations between socialist states.

At the very moment that Khrushchev was praising the power and solidity of the socialist state system, cracks were beginning to appear in its edifice. Behind the challenging Albania stood China, whose leaders openly disapproved both of Russia's condemnation of a small socialist country and the position she took on the question of the inevitability of war. But in their duel, the leadership of the Soviet Union within the socialist system was at stake, and the issue of polycentrism naturally arose. No, the Communist "bloc" was not homogeneous. It, too, suffered from dissensions and contradictions perhaps as serious as any in the Western world.

Khrushchev's confidence, which was affirmed in the new CPSU Program, was no doubt due to the Soviets' conviction that they had considerable military strength, even greater than that of the Western states. But was this the case in reality? Was one to conclude from the Soviets' declarations, from their numerous threats and warnings to the United States and her allies, that there had indeed been a reversal of the balance of power in favor of the U.S.S.R.? It was possible that at the beginning of 1961, the members of the new American Administration felt the United States was indeed lagging behind the U.S.S.R. in military power. But that fear seemed to have dissipated; moreover, the military policy of the previous Republican Administration and of the Macmillan Government, one consequence of which had been a reduction of conventional forces that had dangerously diminished NATO's maneuvering potential in Europe—and the weakness resulting from this policy (aggravated by the use of French forces in Algeria and by the weakness of the Bundeswehr)—had been partially remedied by the end of 1961. The imbalance of conventional forces, significant in the tactical area, was, however, lessened, if not totally compensated for, by the size of the U.S. nuclear-missile stocks. (This arsenal, impressive even in 1960, had been strengthened and reinforced.) If one is to accept a study made by the Institute for Strategic Studies in London, the balance of military strength between the Western allies and the Soviet bloc was rather favorable to the Western powers.*

It was not in the balance of military strength, then, that one could find a valid explanation of the Soviet successes or the Western political defeats. On the contrary, the United States and Europe had not only military but economic power and should have been in a position to prevail over their adversaries. A careful comparison of the two power blocs also did not permit one to conclude that the so-called "socialist" solutions were superior: It was to the West, after all, that the leaders of Communist China and of various East European states turned in order to make ends meet between harvests. And increasing numbers of East Germans sought to reach the territory of the Federal Republic because they were well aware of the different standards of living and the prospects a developing economy offered them. The extent of the progress Russia

SOME COMPARATIVE ESTIMATES OF STRATEGIC STRENGTH
EARLY 1962

CATEGORY	WESTERN ALLIANCES	COMMUNIST BLOC
ICBMs (over 2,000 mile range)	63	50 (min.)
MRBMs (700–2,000 miles range)	186	200
Long-range bombers (over 5,000 mile range)	600	190
Medium-range bombers (over 2,000 mile range, including major carrier-based aircraft)	2200	1100
Battleships and carriers	58	—
Nuclear submarines*	22	2
Conventional submarines	266	480
Cruisers	67	25

* Includes both missile and hunter submarines.

Taken from *The Communist Bloc and the Western Alliances: The Military Balance, 1961–62* (Institute for Strategic Studies: London, 1962). These are only estimates, of course, estimates which, because of the secrecy maintained by military planners—especially in the Soviet Union—must be accepted with reservations.

made under her Communist regime did not lessen the impact of the remarkable results obtained in capitalist countries nor the attraction of an "open" society. Despite the criticisms of what was called the "ugly American," it was nonetheless true that in the balance sheet of economic and financial aid to developing countries, the contribution made by the United States and Europe was undoubtedly greater than that of the Soviet Union and the countries of the Soviet bloc. Nor could attacks against residual colonial imperialism erase the importance of Europe's effort to decolonize at the very time that various Iron Curtain countries were being refused the right of self-determination.

But the Soviet Union was careful to call attention to the successes she brought off; she knew how to exploit her scientific conquests; she was not unaware that the image of the fact counts more than the fact itself and that it is important to predispose public opinion by placing one's policy in a favorable light. More than forty years of experience had given the Soviet leaders real virtuosity in the art of conditioning people. Every political operation was accompanied and covered by a propaganda maneuver that, through the national Communist parties, "front" organizations, press and radio, aimed to orient international public opinion in the desired direction and to create the desired climate of opinion.

The Western powers, who had not yet perfected their techniques of political warfare, were at a loss when faced with these undertakings. The very principles they adhered to limited their freedom either to orient opinion at will or to defend themselves against the intrusions of those who uphold the sacred right to information. There was no more characteristic failure than that of President Kennedy's attempt, after the Cuban affair, to persuade the American press to adopt the self-discipline that he believed to be necessary in the national interest. The Soviet Government, which controlled its news at home but could make wide use of the many sources offered it in the West, enjoyed a real advantage. It could exploit the disagreements of its adversaries, swell the importance of centrifugal forces, or aggravate tensions between the rulers and the ruled in such a way as to reverse the roles and situations, making an aggressor of a victim and imbuing an offensive operation with a defensive character.

These maneuvers were made easier by the pusillanimity of the Western adversaries. The West was hampered not only by its difficulties in mobilizing its economic power for political ends, but also by the consequences of such a mobilization. The Western powers feared both a slow growth of totalitarianism and war; in using the enemy's methods, they ran the risk of destroying the fundamental principles of their society and thereby losing their reasons for defending it. As for the war, they foresaw its consequences too clearly to wish to take any responsibility for it. It is this inability to find a response to the Soviet Union, a response taking account both of Western principles and of the type of struggle imposed by the enemy, that explains the paradoxical contrast between the brilliant dynamism of the West's economy and its inability to seize the political initiative and reverse the current.

Nothing is more certain than that the Western powers were conscious of this contrast. The New Frontier program proved it, as did the many speeches by Kennedy or De Gaulle describing the tasks incumbent on the United States, France, and the West. It was this desire to find a valid reply to what was called the Soviet challenge that animated the participants in the Seventh Annual NATO Parliamentarians' Conference in 1961; they insisted on the need to stand firm on Berlin, to increase the military effort, to strengthen the economic and political unity of the Western world by Great Britain's entry into the Common Market, and, especially, to emphasize the value of scientific and cultural cooperation:

This is a context in which the free world faces a so-called monolithic unity in the communist block of controlled and slave nations. We must be able to match that unity through the institutions of freedom, freely designed by free people. Regardless of the communist threat, this should be done in any case.

The world, which has shrunk in time and space, is facing both new problems and increased opportunities. We face the challenge, not only of getting our own house in order, but also speeding the progress of the peoples of newly developed nations. The new and additional responsibility of members of the Alliance requires determination and unity of purpose. . . .

We believe that the exigencies of the time require consideration of bold, expanded and more advanced methods for bringing about the unity and co-operation which was the spirit of the original Treaty and has been so ever since.*

* Dr. Frans I. Goedhart, "Memorandum of the Political Committee," in NATO Parliamentarians' Conference, *Reports and Recommendations,* Seventh Annual Conference, Paris, November 13–17, 1961, pp. 9–10.

{ 10 }

The Grand Design Debated: 1962

Rarely can a new year have taken over from its predecessor so much unfinished business. Possible further aggressions following that of India against Goa; their effect on the United Nations; Berlin; the Congo; the West's economic progress—in whatever direction one looks nothing has been settled. . . . Yet, given that saving wisdom which can command peoples when they face disaster the outlook need not be gloomy. . . . What the non-communist world is fighting for as a whole and in its parts is cohesion.*

It was this cohesion that the statesmen of Europe and America strove to achieve in the course of the dramatic post-war years. And it was what they continued to strive for in 1962.

In the United States, President Kennedy, faced with his first electoral test since taking office, once again tried to surmount the opposition of conservative forces, whose hold on power was favored by the structure of the American electoral system. Having been elected by only an infinitesimal majority, with only the power of the cities weighing in his

* *The Times* (London), Editorial, January 1, 1962.

favor, Kennedy had come up against a Senate with a strong coalition of Southern Democrats and conservative Republicans, and a House of Representatives whose composition no longer corresponded to the population distribution. His attempts to get the New Frontier program accepted had scarcely more success than in 1961. The resistance by vested interests and a recurrent provincialism had tied him up in a war of attrition in which his appeals to the country, eloquent as they may have been, had no immediate effect. Although the American people had adapted to the world responsibilities imposed on them by World War II, there was still a certain lag between their statesmen's vision of the country's obligations and the local political considerations of many members of Congress. It was only after the passage of time, a change of personnel, revisions of electoral districts (toward which moves were being made in accordance with Supreme Court decisions), that a certain unity of outlook could be re-established.

Similarly, it was to the unity of his people that General de Gaulle never ceased to appeal. But he, too, came up against a number of obstacles, which, far from diminishing, seemed to increase with time. The end of the war in Algeria, which came only after long and laborious negotiations, did not end the struggle for power within France. To the fanaticism of those intent on getting rid of De Gaulle was added a growing impatience on the part of deputies who were even more dissatisfied with the political nursery in which De Gaulle placed them than with his political opinions. And as the President of the Republic chose to attack them directly rather than outmaneuver them, France, at the end of 1962, found herself faced with a new battle on the outcome of which depended not only the fate of De Gaulle's regime but the future of Europe, for France's geographical position made her the pillar of any European structure. Neither the Federal Republic, where Chancellor Adenauer was soon to end his reign, nor Italy, where the "opening to the left" had not resulted in hoped-for political cohesion, nor Great Britain, where Macmillan had just staked his career and his party on Europe, nor the Benelux states could fill the potential void that De Gaulle had filled since 1958.

These internal difficulties, serious as they were and fearful as their repercussions might be, had not retarded Europe's progress toward integration. Various factors contributed to it: Soviet pressure; the economic development of Europe; the feeling that time was limited, and that by entering an international structure, a nation could avoid renewed and destructive nationalism and at the same time resolve its internal problems.

The most vigorous impetus for integration came from the American Government. For the moment seemed to have come to set its cooperation with Europe on a new foundation, the reasons for which President Kennedy explained in his message on trade policy of January 25, 1962:

> The growth of the European Common Market—an economy which may soon nearly equal our own, protected by a single external tariff similar to our own—has progressed with such success and momentum that it has surpassed its original timetable, convinced those initially skeptical that there is now no turning back, and laid the groundwork for a radical alteration of the economics of the Atlantic alliance. Almost 90 per cent of the free world's industrial production (if the United Kingdom and others successfully complete their negotiations for membership) may soon be concentrated in two great markets— the United States of America and the expanded European Economic Community.*

Kennedy then recalled the problems and economic difficulties the United States still had to face: growing pressure on the balance of payments, successive recessions, persistent unemployment, the Soviet economic offensive, the obligation

---

* *A New Foreign Trade Program*, Message of the President to the Congress, transmitted January 25, 1962.

to take account of Japan's needs and expanding economy. It
followed that it was necessary to replace the Reciprocal Trade
Agreement, which was twenty-eight years old, with a new
instrument that was better adapted to the new economic and
political structures of the changing world. This new instrument ought, first of all, to include general powers to allow
for negotiation and reciprocal reductions of up to 50 per cent
on existing tariffs. It ought also to include special powers—
in view of the European Economic Community—to negotiate
for the reduction or even abolition of all tariffs on products
for which the United States and the European Economic
Community account for 80 per cent or more of world
commerce. These products, President Kennedy remarked,
amounted to $2 billion of U.S. exports in 1960 to countries
that would be included in the agreement, and for $1.4 billion
of imports.

The President concluded by emphasizing the symbolic
value of the decision he was asking the Congress to make:

> At rare moments in the life of this nation an opportunity comes
> along to fashion out of the confusion of current events a clear
> and bold action to show the world what it is we stand for. Such
> an opportunity is before us now. This bill, by enabling us to
> strike a bargain with the Common Market, will "strike a blow"
> for freedom.

This radical, almost revolutionary, change of American
economic policy was part of a larger political design—what
was to be called the "Grand Design" which one of the President's closest advisers, McGeorge Bundy, had already presented in a widely publicized speech of December 6, 1961.
After describing the progress of European economic integration and the political purposes of the creation of the Common
Market, Bundy made it clear that United States interest lay in
tying herself not to Great Britain, France, Germany, or Italy
—that is, to states that singly were too weak to counterbalance

the power of America or Russia—but to a politically United Western Europe:

It is of course a hazardous business to predict the form of political relationship which the United States might have with an entity which is only now beginning to come into existence. But my own belief is that the most productive way of conceiving the political future of the Atlantic community is to think in terms of a partnership between the United States, on the one hand, and a great European power, on the other. This partnership would be directed to the constructive and defensive tasks which must be discharged if a genuine community of free nations is to be created: aid to less developed areas, defense against Communist aggression. It would not be an ingrown white man's club; it would rather look outward to larger burdens and opportunities.

Each of these great powers would, of course, have close associates and friends: Canada and the Latin American States on our side, the Commonwealth and the less unified European neighbors on theirs. And they would all be joined together with other free nations in the wide range of common endeavors and enterprises which characterize the free world. Such a partnership makes more sense than a full-blown Atlantic union, which is still constitutionally and psychologically out of range for the people of the United States, and it makes more sense than what we have today. . . .

What I am suggesting, in short, is that the partnership of freedom now requires the re-creation of a great central political force in Western Europe. To this general end Americans of both parties, through three administrations, have given their support, and I believe that history will prove the wisdom of this unbroken purpose.*

* Address to the Economic Club of Chicago, December 6, 1961. In the campaign undertaken by the Kennedy Administration in favor of its trade program, the political intent of the program was strongly emphasized. See George McGhee, Under Secretary for Political Affairs, in the *Department of State Bulletin* (February 19, 1962), p. 289: "The real challenge of the Trade Program lies in the fact that it provides the keystone to our whole forward national strategy, the 'Grand Design' of the world we seek to create."

Bundy's speech is interesting in more than one way. Because of the Common Market's success, the United States was, in fact, in a difficult situation. An economically and politically integrated Europe might become her competitor or even rival; the United States ran the risk of being excluded from a vast protected market and, consequently, of becoming the victim of discrimination on the part of the very states she had encouraged to unite. Great Britain's entry, which she supported, made the problem still greater, since an enlargement of the economic area of Europe might be effected at the expense of the United States. Under these conditions, the American Government might wish to use the opportunity to weld Western Europe and the North American continent into one Atlantic community. But this solution might lead to a relaxation of intra-European ties and consequently to a weakening of Europe's political power. Bundy warned that the Americans were not yet ready to accept such an Atlantic union. And Europeans, in fact, were scarcely more ready than they. Thus, the Grand Design seemed like an attempt to weld together communities that remained distinct but were bound to each other by a common history, by adherence to common values, and by a common interest in protecting themselves against Soviet threats—two communities whose strengths were balanced and complementary.

Encouraging responses to this appeal soon came from Europe. The positive reaction of the Action Committee for the United States of Europe was not surprising. On June 26, 1962, it published a declaration affirming that "The economic and political unity of Europe, including England, and the establishment of European-American relations as between equal partners will alone permit the consolidation of the West and, thus, the creation of the conditions for peace between East and West." Echoing the many declarations that had been

made in the United States in the previous months, the Action
Committee explained:

> Whether it is a question of applying a policy of continued
> economic expansion, of monetary stability in the West, of the
> agricultural problems in more and more industrialized civiliza-
> tions, of aid to underdeveloped countries, of relations with
> countries now becoming industrialized—all these problems can
> be resolved only by Europe and America together, for only
> together do they have the necessary resources.

This opinion was, and the signatures to the declaration bore
witness to the fact, widespread in Western Europe. Many
militant "Europeans" were grateful to the American Government for taking this clear position in favor of the political
integration of the continent. Macmillan, of course, who had
burned his bridges behind him and was now forced to negotiate with the European Economic Community under difficult
conditions, was no less grateful.

But this approval did not in itself solve the many problems.
To the extent that it united politically and economically,
Western Europe could eventually become an equal partner.
But the military issue remained. The Atlantic Alliance had
been born of a common recognition of Europe's incapacity to
assure her own defense by herself. And in the alliance, the
United States, possessing nuclear arms—that is, the strategi-
cally decisive arms—exercised incontestable dominance. Even
if the Europeans, following the American suggestions, made
an effort to strengthen their conventional forces and their total
contribution to NATO, the simple fact that they had neither
atomic weapons nor the power to decide on their use, put
them into a position of inferiority.

For this reason, De Gaulle was unwilling, under present
conditions, to rally to the Grand Design. It was not, as some
of his critics claimed, that he was hostile to the Atlantic Alliance and wanted to break it up. The careful statements he

made at his press conference on May 15, 1962, expressed his belief that French policy objectives included the building up of Europe "in the political, economic, and defense fields," and also "the creation of a modern national army . . . so that, within the framework of a *necessary alliance* and in the hope of an international relaxation, we can, whatever may happen, have our own part in determining our own destiny." A French striking force did not, therefore, imply a position against the Atlantic Alliance; the latter "exists" and "ought to be maintained" as long as the "Soviets threaten the world." Given the new situation, however, the striking force seemed indispensable. Here again, De Gaulle was very precise:

Henceforth, America and Russia will be in a position to strike one another directly and, no doubt, to put one another to death. It is not sure that they will take this risk. No one today can know either when or how one or the other of these great atomic powers will use their nuclear weapons. It suffices to say this to understand that insofar as concerns the defense of France, the battle of Europe, and even a world war, such as they were imagined at the time of NATO's birth, everything is once again open to question.

There was nothing in these declarations that differed from what De Gaulle had previously said to legitimize his creation of an independent nuclear striking force for France. The French Government did not want to accept its exclusion from the atomic club; it declared that it was not satisfied with American assurances concerning nuclear cooperation made to NATO members at the Athens conference early in May, nor with her placing atomic submarines at the disposition of the Atlantic Alliance, all the less so since England was benefiting from her membership in the atomic club. What the French aimed for, in the absence of general disarmament, was, in the field of nuclear weapons as in others, that equality of rights and of capabilities that ought to exist between allies claiming to discuss matters on an equal footing.

American reactions to De Gaulle's declarations were lively, to say the least. The Atlantic Alliance, President Kennedy replied, was not exclusively a function of the Soviet threat, and it was "folly" to fear that the United States might some day renege on promises to defend Europe. It was history more than expedient political choice that led Europe and America to unite. To make doubly clear what he considered was an irreversible movement toward Atlantic unity, President Kennedy, with his characteristic sense of the dramatic, devoted a speech on the anniversary of American independence to a solemn declaration of "interdependence."

In this impassioned dialogue between "Europe from the Atlantic to the Urals" and the "Atlantic Community," it was not the alliance that was in doubt, but the means of collaboration within its framework. That partnership in equality which the promoters of the Grand Design proposed could not be realized so long as the Americans held an atomic monopoly with the English, who, once admitted to the European Economic Community, would be in a privileged position vis-à-vis France. Such was De Gaulle's thesis, to which the Americans replied that they could not enlarge the atomic club without risking a Soviet reaction. To this objection they added another, which Secretary MacNamara revealed in a speech on June 15, when he announced that the United States was now in a position to shelve the policy of massive retaliation and to concentrate the entire range of its atomic weapons on the enemy's military capacity. At the very moment she had finally achieved the flexibility that had been lacking in her policy and strategy, the United States would hardly give to an ally constrained from using massive retaliation by a modesty of means a freedom of action that would compromise her new policies.

But the Grand Design faced not only the atomic obstacle. Its achievement presupposed Europe's political unity. Now, the demands for membership or association successively formulated by the members of the EFTA represented a moral, even political, victory for the European Economic Community, but the great debate within the Europe of the Six over the form to give to possible common political institutions was going on endlessly, and without result. The partisans of "supranational" institutions were opposed by the determined resistance of the French Government, and more particularly by De Gaulle.

Their objective was well enough known. It was a matter of further coordinating the activities of the three communities before proceeding to the election, by universal suffrage, of a European Parliamentary Assembly. In order to succeed, the most rational solution seemed to be the fusion of the three "executives": transferring some of the functions of the ECSC Council of Ministers to the EEC Council and the functions of EURATOM to a single Council of Ministers; in addition, transferring the power of the High Authority and of the EEC Commissions and EURATOM to a single European Commission. This fusion of executives, which would strengthen their influence if not their power, was the substance of the Dutch plan presented in June, 1961. Foreign Minister Luns of the Netherlands, who was at this moment cast in the role of champion of political integration, emphasized that meetings of chiefs of state or of ministers, even if held regularly and even if institutionalized, would not automatically lead to a true and permanent coordination of policies, for ministers are always preoccupied with national problems and are always careful to defend them, since they are responsible to their national legislatures. Thus, their meetings were "ministerial conferences" rather than "councils of ministers."

Luns's relentlessness in defending his "supranational" theses, and his resistance to the French formulas for political collaboration based on regular meetings of heads of governments, may have surprised and even disappointed certain "Europeans" who, being rather more opportunistic, had resigned themselves to a temporary accommodation to the kind of political cooperation the French wanted. But his attitude was a typical defense reflex of a small state toward a "great power" whose decisions might weigh too heavily in the balance. De Gaulle's stubbornness in reaffirming his country's position in relation to her Anglo-Saxon allies, and his tendency to make France the representative and spokesman for all Europe, had given rise to considerable anxiety both on the Continent and in the United States. There had been and still was concern over his tendency to seek an exclusive dialogue with Germany. The small Benelux states—and Italy as well— were resentful and irritated. It was, therefore, in supranational institutions, in the kind of intergovernmental collaboration that progressively reduced national sovereignties, that they sought protection. But the moment Great Britain announced her intention to join the Rome Treaty powers and become a member of the EEC, Dutch and Belgian political leaders were strongly tempted to postpone their solution, the idea being that the adhesion of a third power would re-establish a balance between the great powers and by the same token allow the smaller states a certain degree of freedom.

For, in this debate over political integration, which had placed the so-called French conception of Europe against the plans advocated by those who considered themselves *real* Europeans, everyone was naturally concerned about national independence. The smaller states did not wish to be submerged in a French or Franco-German Europe and sought to build institutions that also would limit the sovereignty of the great powers as well as their own. But faced with the opposition of the French Government, they were led to hope for the entry of Great Britain into the EEC, although there was every possibility that England's admission might strengthen the likelihood of a "Europe of independent states." The contradiction revealed both their anxiety and their difficulty in measuring the economic and political consequences of the Common Market's successes.

De Gaulle took pleasure in noting this contradiction in his press conference of May 15, 1962:

> These opponents say to us on the one hand: "You wish to create a Europe of independent states. We, on the contrary, we want to create a supranational Europe"—as if a formula were sufficient to mix those permanently established entities called peoples and states. They tell us on the other hand: "England has presented her candidacy for entry into the Common Market; so long as she has not joined, we can do nothing political." But everyone knows that England, as a great state and as a nation faithful to herself, would never consent to dissolve herself in some utopian construction.

The attempt to fuse the European executive powers in order to create some "High Authority" working on a majority-rule basis was, in De Gaulle's view, premature and therefore utopian. European reality was still one of sovereign states, and it was dangerous to limit their sovereignty for the benefit of a European government with insufficient means to make its authority respected and therefore threatened with the possibility of becoming the instrument of a "non-European federator." In contrast, De Gaulle restated the essential elements of the proposals France had presented, under the name of the Fouchet Plan, on November 10, 1961. What he saw was a "Union of European States," fairly flexible in its operations, whose heads of state or government, meeting regularly, would administer with the aid of a political commission and the advice of a parliamentary assembly. "After some experience, we shall see in three years what we can do to strengthen our ties. But at least we shall have begun to accustom ourselves to living and acting together."

This pragmatic concept of the new Europe, seductive as it might appear, did not convince the militant "Europeans," no doubt because De Gaulle's concept of the role of the political commission and defense committee he envisioned would compromise the relative independence the European Commission already had and consequently constitute a backward step on the road to integration. But it also failed to convince them because many were unsure of his European convictions, and they interpreted his reticence as evidence of his doubt on the irreversibility of the movement toward Western European integration. The formula "from the Atlantic to the Urals" was distrusted as much in Europe as it was in the United States. For it appeared to reveal De Gaulle's intention not only to "go it alone," but also his desire to assure France a predominant position with the help of Germany.

Logically, ought not "the Europe of independent states" that De Gaulle proposed be open to Great Britain? It was from the French Government that negative responses actually came. The French representative in Brussels offered the greatest number of objections, strictly defended the provisions of the Treaty of Rome, and manifested an intransigeance that was generally interpreted to mean that France wished to keep Great Britain out of Europe. Was this because France was not convinced of the European convictions of the British Government? Or was it rather her desire to hold on to advantages she had acquired only with difficulty? But if this were the case, then why not support the efforts to crown the accomplishments of the EEC with a political structure?

This apparently contradictory attitude gave rise in France to an irritation intensified by resentment of De Gaulle's "splendid isolation." It was not surprising that just when the quarrel between the Executive and the Parliament was poisoning the French political scene, the "Europeans" exploded. In the wake of De Gaulle's press conference of May 15, the MRP members resigned from the government, and, a month later, 293 "European" deputies walked out of the Chamber after reading a manifesto in which they affirmed their desire to see France move along the road of European unity, which they saw "as a democratic community of peoples, and not as a series of conferences in the old-fashioned diplomatic style between governments. . . . We wish the methods and principles that have been successful in the Common Market to be developed and extended to general policy, notably to foreign affairs and defense. We propose the realization, in one or more stages, of the strengthening and fusion of common organisms, the election of a European Assembly by universal suffrage, and the progressive institution of majority-vote decisions in the Council of Ministers." Finally, returning to the Grand Design, they declared: "We reaffirm our conviction that only a United Europe, as an equal partner of the United States within the Atlantic Organization, will be able to preserve the future of our freedom and the future of peace."*

This outburst occurred immediately after an extremely interesting speech by the Minister of Foreign Affairs, a speech to which the rebels had probably not paid much attention, preoccupied as they were with their conflict with the government and their doctrinaire concept of Europe. Couve de Murville had remarked that the doctrinal quarrels dividing the Six were surpassed by fundamental problems posed by the fact that England was at the doors of the Common Market. What would happen if Great Britain were admitted, and, after her, other European states?

Will we always be able to say that this is a regional organization? The weight the Common Market will carry, its network of interests and involvements across the world will be such that it will inevitably become a world system. Its very size will force it to deal on a world scale and to accept what will be a virtual fact of a global trading system, including at least the free world.

If the Common Market is then still Europe, it will be an entirely new Europe. This Europe of the Nine or Ten will be necessarily new, politically speaking. Made up of more dis-

* As reported in *Le Monde* (Paris), June 15, 1962.

parate elements, faced with terrible problems of organization and administration, she will not be able to claim the same degree of cohesion and unity. Possessing more ties to the outside world, she will be more sensitive to outside influences and her policy will be less strictly European.*

Couve de Murville's reflections, which answered the "European" manifesto in advance, admirably defined the European problem of mid-1962. The very successes won by those obscure or famous militants who had been fighting for European unity now forced them once again to pose the original question: Where, then, is Europe? Is it in the complex of France and Germany? Is it to be found in that group of three states—France, Germany, Italy—whose *rapprochement* happened simply in passing? Was it made up of six countries? Or of nine? Or ten? Should Switzerland, the Helvetia Mediatrix that, in the course of centuries, had laboriously built up a collective-security system and acquired experience in federative administration, be excluded? Could Austria be excluded, the Austria that had so miraculously returned to the family of Western nations? Or Finland, which navigated so prudently between two hostile worlds? Was not Europe a continent of special cases? Did she not draw her life's blood from her irreducible diversities?

Attempts were made in vain to set frontiers to a continent that had never had precise boundaries. The undertaking was still more impossible in the twentieth century, when, by virtue of scientific and technological progress, diplomacy had been extended to the entire world and economic activities were ever more inextricably entangled. It was not only North America that wished to strengthen her ties to Europe, but Latin America as well; and Japan; and after Greece, Turkey, Israel, and Iran wanted to become associated. Was it not possible that the rather generous conditions accorded the asso-

* *Ibid.*

ciated states of Africa would encourage similar arrangements? Could one refuse to grant certain members of the Commonwealth the privileges granted to former colonies of France or Belgium? Where was one to stop? And how? On what criteria could one base a selection among states that were European and states that were not? Between measures in the interest of Europe and others? The very success of the European Economic Community incurred the risk that its structure might collapse. Any adhesion to it, any association implied adaptations that, in proportion to the geographic expansion of the Common Market, would bring about still others. And everyone knew that the new U.S. trade policy would not necessarily be limited to the zone covered by the Grand Design.

Thus, at the moment when the achievement of the Grand Design seemed possible, crowning the efforts carried on since the war under the double sign of European and Atlantic union, new obstacles arose. Once more, personal quarrels, doctrinal conflicts, internal complications, economic rivalries, difficulties of defining shifting frontiers clashed with one another, combined, and intensified. Western prosperity contrasted strangely with Europe's chronic political instability, now aggravated by the instability of a world in which the zones of anarchy were widening. Perhaps Europe's difficulties would be attenuated under pressure from the Soviet Union, the country that, since 1945, had been the catalyst of change in Europe and in the Atlantic world, and behind which now stretched the shadow of Communist China.

Epilogue

The last chapters of this essay were written toward the end
of 1962. The referendum campaign was then just beginning
in France. Great Britain was readying herself for another
effort to join the European Economic Community. And the
Americans, with one eye on Cuba and the other on Berlin,
were working to achieve their Grand Design.

A grave crisis in Cuba interrupted these activities. The international socialist camp, whose position was supposed to be
strengthened by this operation, came out of it weakened and
once again divided over its choice of methods and calculation of risks. But the strengthening of the military, political,
and moral position of the United States, whose mastery was
reaffirmed throughout the Cuban crisis, did not lead to the
complete consolidation of the West. After the acrid polemics
that the abandonment of the Skybolt missile had evoked in
Great Britain and the United States, De Gaulle's press conference of January 14, 1963, sharpened the debate that had
begun over the widening frontier of EEC.

The position De Gaulle took was so surprising as to sow
complete confusion and some anger. But his declarations, curt

as they may have been, included nothing he had not already said before. His proposals for the constitution of a three-power directorate were as familiar as his ideas about the organization of Europe. Few were ignorant of his reservations over an Atlantic military force that would allow Great Britain to retain her privileged atomic position; his desire to give France an independent nuclear striking force was also known. But it had not been imagined—and in this his stubbornness was underestimated—that he would go so far as to risk a break in the Atlantic Alliance.

But the break, if one looks at it from a historical perspective, was perhaps not so threatening as it was imagined then. More than once since 1945, the ties woven among European states and across the Atlantic had almost been broken. And each time the pressure of circumstances had forced all parties to maintain and even strengthen them. Moreover, the argument that De Gaulle was deliberately seeking a break in order to affirm French leadership and to prepare for some undisclosed reversal of alliances had no serious basis in fact. At each of his press conferences, he had taken care to emphasize the value, even the necessity, of the Atlantic Alliance: "It is obvious that a country such as our own cannot now, would not now be able to, fight a great modern war alone. It goes without saying that, given the historical period in which we live, we must have allies."

As far as Great Britain was concerned, De Gaulle did not fail to underscore the strength and importance of the ties that, despite everything, bound her to France and the Continent. "It is, then, possible that England will one day transform herself sufficiently to become part of the European Community without restriction or reservation, and in preference to anything else; in that case, the Six will open the door to her, and France will not stand in the way."

Nor was there anything in De Gaulle's remarks to suggest that he was thinking of an agreement with the U.S.S.R.

Those who thought so were forgetting that in December, 1944, when accused of disloyalty to the Western Alliance, he showed himself more intransigent on the question of self-determination for Poland than did Roosevelt and Churchill at Yalta a few weeks later. They were also forgetting his firmness at the time of the Berlin crisis. His attitude to the U.S.S.R. was, in fact, scarcely different from that of his American allies: firm on the fundamental questions and at the same time sufficiently flexible to take account of an evolution (which a truly correct policy will never exclude, no matter how problematical it may be) of Soviet policy.

Rather than seek explanations for De Gaulle's policy in wounds to his self-esteem or in some secret design, it would be more worthwhile to examine the reasons he himself advanced for his opposition to the entry of Great Britain into the European Economic Community. Certain passages of his January 14 declaration are significant and revealing in this regard, for instance, his reminder that the solidarity of the Six was due particularly to the fact "that none of them is tied to the outside by any special political or military agreement." After examining the hypothesis of Great Britain's entry, he said, "It is conceivable that the cohesion of the many and most diverse members [of an enlarged Community] will not long endure and that, in the final analysis, there will appear a colossal Atlantic Community dependent on, and directed by, America and which would soon absorb the European Community." He added immediately, "This is a hypothesis that can be perfectly well justified to some, but it is not what France wanted to do nor what she is doing, which is the development of a European structure properly so called."

De Gaulle's opposition to a multilateral armed force came from the same intention not to allow an Atlantic Community under American direction to absorb the European Community. It was not due to hostility to the United States, but rather to a wish to retain the freedom of acting on the destiny of Europe and of France in case the United States were not in a position to do so.

Could this logical and cold argumentation convince De Gaulle's audience, who were sensitive to the power of myths but who had been not only surprised but hurt by him before? To what extent could it influence a public that easily allowed itself the luxury of national emotion? At the moment these lines are being written, De Gaulle remains isolated. He is isolated in France, where his enemies are many and where his independent French striking force is meeting with vigorous opposition. He is isolated in Europe, where Chancellor Adenauer has left his place to men less willing than he to restrict themselves within the confines of a Franco-German dialogue. He is no better understood in Belgium or in Italy than in England. His American allies remind him, not without justification, that they are still carrying most of the burden of Europe's defense, and that without great effort, which she did not wish and was not in a position to make, Europe would be unable to relieve her of this responsibility without endangering her very existence.

But these national positions are not perhaps so far apart as they may seem at first. By insisting that Great Britain renounce her special alliances and, above all, her special ties to the United States as the condition of her entry into the European Economic Community, De Gaulle in fact favored the realization of the Grand Design. For only a group including the United Kingdom as well as France and Germany can create the counterweight necessary in order that Europe may become the "equal partner" the United States desires. But British participation inevitably means a transformation of the Community. With Great Britain included, a Europe cut off from the East is inevitably an Atlantic Europe. It is not so much interdependence that is subject to question as the forms of European or Atlantic cooperation. This does not mean that the problems will be less difficult to resolve. Whether it is a question of European or American tariffs, of the strength of the dollar, or of the right to use atomic weapons, essential interests are at stake. By intervening as he has, De Gaulle not only put the brake on European integration, but hardened contradictions among these erstwhile allies that have yet to be proved surmountable.

Geneva
Summer, 1963

A Selected
Bibliography

A Selected
Bibliography

1. OFFICIAL DOCUMENTS

FRANCE. *Journal officiel de la République française.*
GERMANY. *Verhandlungen des Deutsches Bundestages.*
GREAT BRITAIN. *Parliamentary Debates* (Hansard).
UNITED STATES. *Congressional Record.*

COMITÉ D'ACTION POUR LES ETATS-UNIS D'EUROPE. *Déclarations communes.* Paris.
COMITÉ INTERGOUVERNEMENTAL CRÉÉ PAR LA CONFÉRENCE DE MESSINE. *Rapport des chefs de délégations aux ministres des affaires étrangères.* Brussels, 1956.
CONGRESS OF EUROPE. *Verbatim Report.* The Hague, 1949.
COUNCIL OF EUROPE, CONSULTATIVE ASSEMBLY. *Reports, Agendas, Minutes, and Working Papers.* Strasbourg, 1949–62.
EUROPEAN FREE TRADE ASSOCIATION. *The Stockholm Convention and Freer World Trade.* Stockholm, 1959.
NORTH ATLANTIC TREATY ORGANIZATION, COUNCIL. *Ministerial Meetings.* Paris.
———, PARLIAMENTARIANS' CONFERENCES. *Reports and Recommendations.* Paris.
ORGANIZATION FOR EUROPEAN ECONOMIC COOPERATION. *A Decade of Cooperation: Achievements and Perspectives.* Paris, 1958.
———. *A Remodeled Economic Organisation: A Report by the Group of Four.* Paris, April, 1960.
———. *Report on the possibility of creating a free trade area.* Paris, January, 1957.

ACHESON, DEAN. *Strengthening the Forces of Freedom: Selected Speeches and Statements of Secretary of State Acheson: February, 1949–April, 1950.* Washington, D.C.: Government Printing Office, 1950.

CHURCHILL, SIR WINSTON S. *Europe Unite: Speeches, 1947-48.* London: Cassell & Company, 1950.

———. *The Second World War.* Vol. II: *Their Finest Hour.* London: Cassell & Company, 1949; Boston: Houghton Mifflin Company, 1950.

———. *The Sinews of Peace: Postwar Speeches.* London: Cassell & Company, 1948.

DE GAULLE, CHARLES. *Discours de guerre, 1940–45.* 2 vols. Paris: Egloff, 1944–45.

———. *The Speeches of General de Gaulle.* London and New York: Oxford University Press, 1944.

ISMAY, LORD. *NATO, The First Five Years, 1949–54.* Paris: NATO, 1955.

KHRUSHCHEV, NIKITA S. *Documents of the Twenty-second Congress of the Communist Party of the Soviet Union.* Vol. I: *Report on the World Situation;* Vol. II: *Report on the Program of the Communist Party of the Soviet Union.* New York: Crosscurrents Press, 1961.

PASSERON, ANDRÉ (ed.). *De Gaulle parle.* Paris: Plon, 1962.

SHERWOOD, ROBERT E. *Roosevelt and Hopkins: An Intimate History.* New York: Harper & Brothers, 1950. Published in London by Eyre and Spottiswoode under the title *The White House Papers of Harry L. Hopkins: An Intimate History.*

American Foreign Policy, 1950–56, Basic Documents. Washington, D.C.: Government Printing Office, 1957.

COLLIARD, CLAUDE ALBERT. *Droit international et histoire diplomatique: Documents choisis.* Paris: Domat Montchrestien, 1950.

Czechoslovak sources and documents. New York: Czechoslovak Information Service.

A Decade of American Foreign Policy, Basic Documents, 1941–49. Washington, D.C.: Government Printing Office, 1950.

Department of State Bulletin. Washington, D. C.

La Documentation française: Articles et documents. Paris.

La Documentation française: Notes et études documentaires. Paris.

Documents on International Affairs: 1949–50. London: Oxford University Press, 1953.

Economic Survey of Europe. Geneva: United Nations Economic Commission for Europe.

The New Communist Manifesto and Related Documents. 2d ed. Evanston, Ill.: Row, Peterson, 1962.

2. NEWSPAPERS AND PERIODICALS

Bulletin of the Centre Européen de la Culture, Geneva.
The Economist, London.
Foreign Affairs, New York.
Foreign Policy Reports, Washington.
International Affairs, London.
Neue Zürcher Zeitung, Zurich.
The New York Times, New York.
Le Monde, Paris.
La Revue d'histoire de la deuxième guerre mondiale, Paris.
Revue française de science politique, Paris.

3. STUDIES

British Security: A Report by a Chatham House Study Group. London and New York: Royal Institute of International Affairs, 1946.
CATLIN, GEORGE. *The Atlantic Community.* London: Coram, 1959.
The Communist Bloc and the Western Alliances: The Military Balance, 1961–62. London: Institute for Strategic Studies, 1962.
COUDENHOVE-KALERGI, RICHARD. *An Idea Conquers the World.* London: Hutchinson & Co., 1953.
L'Esprit européen. Published for Rencontres internationales de Genève, 1946. Neuchâtel: Editions de la Baconnière, 1947.
L'Europe de demain, published by the Centre d'action pour la fédération européenne. Neuchâtel: Éditions de la Baconnière, 1945.
France and Britain: A Report by a Chatham House Study Group. London: Royal Institute of International Affairs, 1945.
FREYMOND, JACQUES. *The Saar Conflict: 1945–55.* London: Stevens & Sons; New York: Frederick A. Praeger, 1960.
GERBET, PIERRE. "Genèse du Plan Schuman," *Revue française de science politique*, July–September, 1956.
HAYES, CARLTON. "The American Frontier—Frontier of What?," *American Historical Review*, LI, January, 1946.
"Hommage à un grand Européen: Joseph H. Retinger," *Bulletin* of the Centre Européen de la Culture, No. 5, 1960–61.
LAYTON, SIR WALTER. *The British Commonwealth and World Order.* Sidney Ball Lecture, March 3, 1944 (Barnett House Papers, No. 27). London: Oxford University Press, 1944.
MICHEL, HENRI, and MIRKINE-GUETZEVITCH, BORIS. *Les idées politiques et sociales de la Résistance en France: Documents clandestins, 1940–44.* Paris: Presses Universitaires de France, 1954.
NOËL, LÉON. "Le projet d'union franco-britannique de juin 1940," *La Revue d'histoire de la deuxieme guerre mondiale*, January, 1956, pp. 22–37.

"Non-Military Cooperation in NATO," *NATO Letters,* Vol. V, Special Supplement No. 1, section 15 (January, 1957).

PHILIP, OLIVIER. *Le problème de l'union européenne.* Neuchâtel: Editions de la Baconnière, 1950.

PIRENNE, JACQUES, and PIRENNE, JACQUES-HENRI. *La Belgique devant le nouvel équilibre du monde.* Brussels: C. Dessart, 1944.

"Le Projet de marché commun européen," *Bulletin de la Confédération nationale du patronat français* (Paris), Supplement to No. 153 (1956).

ROBERTSON, A. H. *The Council of Europe: Its Structure, Functions, and Achievements.* 2d ed. London: Stevens & Sons; New York: Frederick A. Praeger, 1961.

DE ROUGEMONT, DENIS. *L'Europe en jeu.* Neuchâtel: Editions de la Baconnière, 1948.

———. *Vingt-huit siècles d'Europe.* Paris: Payot, 1961.

STREIT, CLARENCE. *Union Now.* London: Jonathan Cape; New York: Harper & Brothers, 1939.

VALÉRY, PAUL. *Regards sur le monde actuel.* Paris: Gallimard, 1945.

Index

Name Index

Acheson, Dean, 61–62
Adenauer, Konrad, 45, 78, 79, 82, 96, 99, 110, 113, 116, 165–68, 171, 186, 187, 201, 219
Armstrong, Hamilton Fish, 69–70
Attlee, Clement, 52, 96, 115

Bastid, Paul, 37
Bem, General, 120
Berle, Adolf, 37
Bernstein, Eduard, 64
Bevin, Ernest, 45, 52, 55, 56, 62
Blum, Léon, 51, 64
Bonnefous, Edouard, 81
Bourdet, Claude, 75–76
Bourguiba, Habib, 118
Brandt, Willy, 187
Briand, Aristide, 6
Brogan, Denis, 66
Brugmans, Henri, 46
Bulganin, Nikolai, 113
Bundy, McGeorge, 203–5
Butler, Sir Harold, 37, 115
Byrnes, James, 101

Carr, E. H., 14
Castro, Fidel, 178
Chiang Kai-shek, General, 71, 105
Churchill, Winston, 6, 8, 13, 15, 16, 23, 26, 29, 30, 34–37, 39, 44, 45, 46, 50, 80, 96, 218
Commin, Pierre, 130

Corbin, Charles, 8
Coudenhove-Kalergi, Richard, 6, 17, 37, 53
Courtin, René, 37
Couve de Murville, Maurice, 213–14

Dautry, Raoul, 37
Debré, Michel, 37
De Gasperi, Alcide, 51
De Gaulle, Charles, 8, 17, 18, 32, 146, 148, 149, 150, 160, 162, 182, 183, 185, 198, 201, 202, 206–9, 210–12, 216–20
Dennery, Etienne, 7
Duhamel, Georges, 65
Dulles, John Foster, 39, 105, 106, 114, 119, 120, 124, 165

Eden, Anthony, 12, 98
Eisenhower, Dwight D., 90, 95, 102, 104, 106, 115, 116, 141–42, 161
Erhard, Ludwig, 96, 151, 160

Fanfani, Amintore, 130
Frenay, Henri, 9

Gilson, Etienne, 68, 75
Giscard d'Estaing, Valéry, 37
Guesde, Jules, 64

Hammarskjöld, Dag, 190
Harriman, Averell, 37

Hayes, Carlton, 66
Heath, Edward, 164
Heuss, Theodor, 78
Hiss, Alger, 71, 101
Hitler, Adolf, 6, 11, 24, 25
Hoffman, Paul, 84
Hoover, Herbert, 88, 89, 124
Ho Chi Minh, 97

Jaspers, Karl, 21
Jaurès, Jean, 64
Jenner, William E., 103

Kautsky, Karl, 64
Kennan, George, 139
Kennedy, John F., 173–76, 179, 184,
    185, 197, 198, 200–203, 209
Kennedy, Joseph, 89
Kiesinger, Kurt, 130
Khrushchev, Nikita, 113, 114, 139,
    165, 170, 171, 173, 184, 185, 187,
    188, 191, 193

Layton, Sir Walter, 23
Lecourt, Robert, 130
Lenin, V. I., 60, 63
Lippmann, Walter, 26
Lovett, Robert, 56
Lukacs, George, 22
Luns, J. M. A. H., 209

MacArthur, Douglas, 101
McCarthy, Joseph, 103
Macmillan, Harold, 37, 46, 126, 171,
    180, 181, 185, 195, 202, 206
MacNamara, Robert, 208
Malagodi, Giovanni, 130
Mann, Thomas, 11
Mao Tse-tung, 71
Marshall, George C., 40, 55
Marx, Karl, 22, 64
Matteotti, Matteo, 130
Maudling, Reginald, 164
Mayer, René, 99
Mauriac, François, 65
Mendès-France, Pierre, 106–8, 111
Mollet, Guy, 126
Molotov, V. M., 16, 31, 42
Monick, Emmanuel, 8
Monnet, Jean, 8, 50, 83, 84, 128, 129,
    136, 161

Mussolini, Benito, 33

Nagy, Imre, 120
Nasser, Gamal Abdel, 117, 119–20,
    122
Nenni, Pietro, 75
Nixon, Richard, 171

Ollenhauer, Erich, 130

Pearson, Lester, 61, 71
Peter the Great, 22
Philip, André, 81
Philip, Olivier, 46
Pirenne, Jacques, 28
Pleven, René, 85–86, 130
Proudhon, Pierre Joseph, 64

Ramadier, Paul, 37
Reston, James, 68
Retinger, Joseph, 36, 45, 51
Reynaud, Paul, 37, 46, 47
Roosevelt, Franklin D., 17, 18, 23,
    24, 25, 29, 30, 90, 175, 218
Rougemont, Denis de, 21

Saint Laurent, Louis, 55
Salan, General, 145
Sandys, Duncan, 45, 51
Sartre, Jean-Paul, 65
Schmid, Carlo, 169
Schumacher, Kurt, 79, 168, 169
Schuman, Robert, 62, 80, 82, 99, 134,
    149
Serruy, Daniel, 37
Sidi ben Youssef, 118
Siegfried, André, 37
Sikorski, General, 36
"Sirius," 67–68
Smuts, Jan Christian, Marshal, 14
Soloviev, Colonel, 189
Spaak, Paul-Henri, 42, 51, 129, 130,
    132–34, 142
Spender, Stephen, 21
Stalin, Joseph, 18, 24, 29, 31, 66, 104,
    114, 121
Stevenson, Adlai, 102
Strait, Clarence, 8, 26

Taft, Robert, 103
Teitgen, Pierre-Henri, 37
Thorneycroft, Peter, 37

Tocqueville, Alexis de, 65
Toynbee, Arnold, 7
Truman, Harry S., 56, 59, 75, 101, 102, 115

Ulbricht, Walter, 184, 186

Valéry, Paul, 20

Vandenberg, Arthur, 56
Vansittart, Sir Robert, 8
Van Zeeland, Paul, 36

Watson, General, 189
Wehner, Herbert, 130
Willkie, Wendell, 25
Wilson, Woodrow, 68

Subject Index

Africa, 17, 24, 72, 89, 117, 119, 124, 140, 144, 178, 215

Albania, 195

Algeria, 118–19, 122, 126, 143, 144–46, 165, 173, 182–84, 195, 201; *see also* FLN, OAS

Alliance for Progress, 178, 179

Allied Powers, 7, 14, 18, 19, 31–33, 54–55, 79

Asia, 20, 23, 86, 117, 119, 123, 124, 125, 178; *see also* Southeast Asia

Atlantic Charter, 25, 27

Atlantic Conference (Bruges, 1957), 142

Austria, 3, 15, 113, 135, 151, 154, 167, 214

Balkan states, 11–12, 18, 34

Baltic Sea, 12

Belgium, 27, 37, 50, 100, 108, 154, 210, 215, 219

Benelux states, 128, 151, 160, 202, 210

Berlin, 54–55, 58, 78, 101, 104, 139, 165, 170, 172, 184–89, 198, 200, 216, 218

Bolshevism, 4, 22, 25

British Commonwealth, 14–15, 23, 25, 26, 27, 35, 44, 52, 53, 123, 135, 181, 204, 215

Brussels Treaty, 44, 52, 55, 56, 73, 108–9

Burma, 97

Canada, 55, 59, 61, 71, 93, 162, 163, 204

Central Powers, 4

China, 5

China, People's Republic of, 86, 87, 88, 97, 101, 106, 119, 143, 193, 195, 196, 215

Christian Democratic parties, European, 37, 64

Christian Democratic Party (Union), German, 78, 79, 99, 166, 167, 168, 188

College of Europe (Bruges), 54

Common Market, *see* EEC

Communist parties, European, 4, 34–35, 43, 63, 71, 74, 86, 98, 101, 103, 104, 116, 127, 173

Communist Party, French, 32, 33, 100

Communist Party of the Soviet Union: Twentieth Congress of, 114, 116, 191, 192; Twenty-second Congress of, 191–95; *see also* Marxism–Leninism

Congo, 200

Congress of Europe (The Hague, 1948), 42, 45–49, 50, 81, 130

Conservative Party, British, 44, 52, 96, 115, 116, 126

Council of Europe, 13, 52–53, 79, 81, 82, 84, 98–99, 113, 130, 136

Cuba, 178–79, 197, 216

Cyprus, 117, 118
Czechoslovakia, 11, 12, 13, 16, 35, 42, 43, 54, 67, 171

Democratic Party, U.S., 115, 175, 201
Denmark, 11, 59, 92, 95, 154, 157

Eastern Europe, 4, 12, 15, 16, 20, 31, 35, 36, 42, 43, 112, 121, 184, 189, 196
Economic League for European Co-operation, 45
EDC (European Defense Community), 92, 98, 99–101, 105, 106, 107–8, 110, 112, 116–17, 131, 138
EEC (European Economic Community), 98, 133, 134, 135, 136, 137, 138, 148, 149, 150, 154, 155, 156–57, 158, 159, 160, 161, 162, 164, 181, 198, 202–3, 205, 206, 208, 209, 210, 211, 213–14, 215, 216, 218, 219
EFTA (European Free Trade Association), 157–64, 209
EURATOM (European Atomic Energy Commission), 129, 131, 133, 134, 148, 209
European Coal and Steel Community (ECSC), 80–84, 98, 100, 128, 131, 133, 148, 209
European Cultural Center (Geneva), 54
European Cultural Conference (Lausanne, 1949), 54
European Movement, 50–51, 53–54, 70; Brussels Congress (1949), 53; Westminster Congress (1949), 53, 81
European Parliamentary Union, 37; first congress of (Gstaad, 1947), 37–38
European Payments Union, 135, 154
European Recovery Program, 70
European Union of Federalists, 38, 45; Montreux Congress (1947), 38–39, 80–81

Finland, 191, 214
FLN, 144, 182
Formosa, 104–5, 143
France, 3, 4, 5, 13, 14, 24, 32, 35, 37, 43, 54, 71 80, 83, 89, 92, 97, 106–8,

112, 116, 118, 121, 122, 124, 126, 134, 143–50, 160, 165, 166, 173, 182–84, 198, 210, 214, 215, 217, 219; and Europe, 9–10, 17–18, 52, 83–84, 99, 108–9, 129, 134, 136, 148–49, 154, 155, 160, 165, 210–14, 216–20; and Germany, 78, 80, 82, 85–86, 99, 100, 116, 149, 166, 210, 212, 219; and Great Britain, 6–9, 14, 26, 44–45, 138, 149, 210–14, 217–20; and NATO, 95, 97, 108, 149, 217–18; and the Soviet Union, 217–18; and the United States, 62, 65–66, 67–68, 92, 97–98, 105, 106, 108, 116, 140–41, 149, 203, 206–8, 210, 213, 218–19
French Committee for European Federation, 9–10
French Council for a United Europe, 37, 45

German Democratic Republic (D.D.R.), 79, 166, 169, 184, 185, 186, 188, 191, 196
Germany, 3; occupied, 18, 20, 31–32, 35, 36, 46, 54; Third Reich, 5, 7, 9, 11, 13, 14, 90, 188; see also Berlin
Germany, Federal Republic of, 69, 75, 76, 78–79, 90, 96–97, 100, 108, 109, 110, 134, 154, 165–69, 173, 186, 189, 196, 201, 210, 214; and Europe, 98, 109–10, 129, 134, 150–51, 160, 165; and France, 80–83, 86, 116–17, 138, 149, 165, 210, 212; and Great Britain, 78, 85, 165; and the Soviet Union, 79, 86, 110, 112, 165, 166, 169, 184, 186–88; and the United States, 110, 116, 165, 166, 203
Goa, 181, 191, 200
Great Britain, 3, 4, 5, 13, 16, 17, 18, 19, 24, 25, 37, 71, 72, 87, 88, 97, 117, 121, 122, 123, 126–27, 154, 166, 173, 180–82, 202, 207; and Europe, 12, 13–15, 18, 19, 23–24, 42, 44–45, 52–53, 55, 100, 109, 135, 138, 150, 151, 154, 157, 160, 164, 181, 198, 205, 210–12, 213, 216; and France, 6–9, 14, 26, 44–45, 138, 149, 165, 181, 210–14, 217–20; and Germany, 78, 85, 165; and NATO, 95, 195, 198, 207; and the Soviet Union, 15, 16, 31, 34–35,

165, 181; *see also* British Commonwealth

Greece, 11, 12, 13, 20, 34, 39–40, 68, 95, 101, 118, 125, 135, 154, 214

Guinea, 147

Hiroshima, 28

Hungary, 171; Revolution of 1956, 120–21, 122, 123, 126, 127, 134

Iceland, 135

India, 87, 97, 121, 191, 200

Indochinese war, 71, 85, 97, 106, 118, 145, 177; *see also* Vietminh, Vietnam

Indonesia, 97, 191

Iran, 35, 214

Iraq, 117, 143

Ireland, 59, 135, 154

Israel, 121, 122, 214

Italy, 20, 33, 35, 37, 40, 43, 54, 64, 69, 72, 90, 95, 96, 100, 108, 116, 129, 134, 151, 154, 201, 203, 210, 214, 219; Fascist, 5, 10, 11, 13

Japan, 5, 14, 113, 177, 203, 214

Jordon, 117

Kashmir, 181

Kenya, 181

Korean War, 76–77, 85–89, 93, 101, 104–5, 139

Laos, 177, 180, 184

Labour Party, British, 23, 34, 44, 45, 52, 72, 88, 96, 115, 116

Latin America, 89, 117, 177, 178, 179–80, 204, 214; *see also* Alliance for Progress, Rio Pact

League of Nations, 13, 26

Lebanon, 143

Liberal Party, German, 79

Lorraine, 82

Luxembourg, 37

Madagascar, 147

Mahgreb, 118

Marshall Plan, 40–42, 43, 45, 46, 63, 101, 161, 177

Marxism-Leninism, 31, 63, 114, 122, 194

Middle East, 72, 117, 121, 122, 123, 124, 126, 181; *see also* Suez crisis

Monnet Plan, 83-84

Morocco, 18–19, 144

Mukden incident, 6

Munich Pact, 4, 171

NATO, 59–63, 74, 77, 85, 87, 91, 92–96, 97, 108, 109, 110, 112, 118, 119, 125, 126, 138, 141, 142, 149, 161, 162, 165, 170, 177, 184, 195, 206, 207; bases, 119; Committee of Economic and Financial Defense, 74, 93; Committee on Nonmilitary Cooperation ("Three Wise Men's" Report), 139–40; Council, 74, 77, 93, 99–100, 109, 139, 142; forces, 74, 90; Lisbon Conference (1952), 93–94, 100; Military (Defense) Committee, 74, 93; Military Production Committee, 74; Ottawa Conference (1951), 93; Parliamentarian's Conference (1957), 142; Parliamentarian's Conference (1961), 198–99; Treaty, 61, 66, 67, 69, 70, 72, 73, 75, 89, 90, 95, 99, 108, 110, 118, 125, 140, 148, 199

Neman, 22

Netherlands, 11, 37, 97, 100, 108, 160, 191, 209, 210

Nordic federation, 18

North Africa, 122

Norway, 11, 27, 59, 95, 154, 157; *see also* Nordic federation, Scandinavia

OAS, 182–83

OEEC (Organisation for European Economic Cooperation), 78, 84, 135, 138, 150, 152–53, 162, 163

Paris Agreements (1954), 109, 110, 112, 116

Poland, 11, 12, 13, 16, 120, 171, 218

Portugal, 59, 92, 135, 151, 157

Potsdam Agreements, 31

Prussia, 3

Radical Party, French, 107

Rapallo Treaty, 79

Rencontres Internationales (Geneva, 1946), 21–22
Republican Party, U.S., 39, 89, 101, 115, 175, 201
Resistance movements, 9, 10, 11, 32, 63
Rhine, Rhineland, 4, 22, 69
Rhodesia, 181
Rio Pact (1948), 56
Rome Treaty (1957), 134, 135, 136, 149, 157, 160, 161, 164, 182, 210, 212
Ruhr, 82
Russia, 3, 25, 28; see also Soviet Union

Saar, 80, 82, 116–17, 169
Sahara Desert, 144
Scandinavia, 135, 151
Schuman Plan, 80–84, 85, 98, 138
SEATO, 177
Social Democratic Party, German, 79, 99, 167, 168, 169, 171
Socialist Party, French, 32, 33, 107
Southeast Asia, 106, 177, 180
Soviet Union, 5, 15, 18–19, 22, 31, 34, 35, 43, 60–61, 66, 72, 75, 76, 77, 78, 86, 89, 97, 114, 117, 119, 121, 124, 132, 139, 141, 148, 173, 177, 181, 191–94, 195, 202, 204; and Eastern Europe, 15–16, 31, 121, 123, 126–27; and France, 217–18; and Germany, 18–19, 54–55, 79, 86, 109–10, 112, 165–66, 167, 169, 184, 186–88; and Great Britain, 15, 16, 31, 34–35, 165, 181; and the United States, 16, 39, 43, 60, 75, 77, 105, 115, 141, 184–86, 195; and the West, 16, 31, 33–34, 42, 43, 54, 60–61, 79, 101, 114, 117, 123, 125, 126–27, 165, 184, 195–99
Spain, 90, 135
Straits, the, 34
Suez Canal crisis, 112, 117, 119–20, 121, 122, 127, 134, 136, 138
Sweden, 154, 157; see also Nordic federation, Scandinavia
Switzerland, 135, 151, 154, 157, 214
Syria, 191
Stockholm Appeal, 74

Tehran Conference, 29
Thailand, 180
Truman Doctrine, 39–40
Tunisia, 107, 118–19, 144
Turkey, 34, 35, 39–40, 69, 96, 101, 118, 125, 135, 214

Union of South Africa, 181
United Europe Movement, 37, 45
United Nations, 29, 31, 44, 55, 57, 60, 61, 86, 88, 113, 123, 124, 125, 143, 177, 178, 188, 189–91 200; Charter, 44, 55, 56, 57, 58, 62, 69, 190; Economic Commission for Europe, 153; Security Council, 55
United States, 4, 5, 7, 15, 16, 18, 21, 24–27, 34, 35, 40, 44, 56–59, 66–68, 71, 73, 75, 83, 85, 86, 90, 92, 101–6, 114–17, 120, 124, 125, 132, 142, 143, 155, 162, 170, 172, 173, 174–80, 181, 185, 191, 193, 196–97, 198, 200–201, 203–5, 206, 208, 213, 215, 216, 219; and the Atlantic Community, 26–28; and Europe, 16, 23, 30, 31, 39, 40–42, 54–59, 61–62, 68–69, 71, 73, 87–91, 99, 114, 119, 135, 155, 160–63, 191, 202–5, 214; and France, 62, 65–66, 67–68, 92, 97–98, 105, 106, 108, 116, 140–41, 149, 203, 206–8, 210, 213, 218–19; and Germany, 116, 165, 166, 203; and Great Britain, 25–26, 27, 39, 55, 62, 88–89, 105, 120, 124, 140–41, 143, 165, 181, 203, 208, 219; and the Middle East, 124–27; and NATO, 59–62, 67, 92–96, 119, 125, 162, 206, 208; and the Soviet Union, 16, 35, 39, 43, 60, 75, 77, 105, 115, 141, 184–86, 195; European views on, 23, 62–66, 87
United States of Europe, 35, 37, 40, 101, 131; Action Committee for, 130–35, 205; Socialist Movement for, 51
Urals, 22, 208, 212

Vandenberg Revolution, 56–69
Vatican, 33
Versailles Treaty, 4
Vietminh, 97

Vietnam, 180
Vistula, 22

Wall Street crash, 6, 65
Warsaw Pact, 112

World War I, 4
World War II, 85, 146, 201

Yalta Agreements, 31, 101, 218
Yugoslavia, 11, 12, 13, 113

DATE DUE

APR 4 '67			
APR 18 '67			
MAY 1 '67			
FEB 28 '68			
FEB 21 70			
APR 21 '70			
APR 2 '71			
APR 19 '71			
FEB 24 '72			
APR 12 '72			
APR 26 72 NO 24 '81			
GAYLORD			PRINTED IN U.S.A